For Bill

Best wishes

Larry B Massie

Also by Larry B. Massie

The Allure of Michigan's Past (2008)
This Place Called Portage (2006)
Brown & Golden Memories (2003)
A Grand Adventure (2001)
White Pine Whispers (1998)
Haven, Harbor & Heritage (1996)
On the Road to Michigan's Past (1995)
Michigan Memories (1994)
Birchbark Belles (1993)
Potawatomi Tears & Petticoat Pioneers (1992)
The Romance of Michigan's Past (1991)
Walnut Pickles & Watermelon Cake (1990) *with Priscilla Massie*
Pig Boats & River Hogs (1990)
Copper Trails & Iron Rails (1989)
Voyages Into Michigan's Past (1988)
Warm Friends & Wooden Shoes (1988)
From Frontier Folk to Factory Smoke (1987)
Battle Creek: The Place Behind the Product (1984) *with Peter Schmitt*
Kalamazoo: The Place Behind the Product (1981) *with Peter Schmitt*

TWO-TRACKS TO MICHIGAN'S PAST

One of Mackinac Island's famous attractions, Sugar Loaf Rock, as depicted in a Great Lakes shipping promotional guide, ca. 1890.

TWO-TRACKS TO MICHIGAN'S PAST

BY
LARRY B. MASSIE

The Priscilla Press
Allegan Forest, Michigan
2009

Copyright 2009 by Larry B. Massie
Cover illustration is of a two-track in the Allegan
Forest photographed by author in Spring 2009.

All rights are reserved.
No portion of this publication may
be reproduced without the express
permission of the author.

Please direct any questions or comments
concerning this publications to:
Priscilla Massie
2109 41st Street
Allegan Forest, MI. 49010
(269) 673-3633

ISBN - 978-1-886167-30-8

*For Dr. Philip P. Mason,
my friend, whose career is an
inspiration for historians, archivists and
bookmen of my generation and many
more to come.*

TABLE OF CONTENTS

Preface... 11

CHAPTER I
    Michigan's First Christmas Celebration 13

CHAPTER II
    The Moore-Hascall Dream Machine 24

CHAPTER III
    Dr. Goodrich, Allegan County's
    Pioneer Physician............................ 34

CHAPTER IV
    "The Wildest & Tenderest Piece of Beauty
    On God's Earth"............................. 40

CHAPTER V
    Talking with the Dead 62

CHAPTER VI
    Scientists in the North Country 72

CHAPTER VII
    When Christmas Was Just Another Day 82

CHAPTER VIII
    The Husseys of Battle Creek 95

CHAPTER IX
    The Drummer Boy of Chickamauga 105

CHAPTER X
    Chaplain Corby of the Irish Brigade 113

CHAPTER XI
    Book Hawkers & Door Knockers 124

CHAPTER XII
    Agassiz Redux & Red Rock Riches............ 138

CHAPTER XIII
    As the Bishop Saw It 149

Chapter XIV
    Johnston's Got Your Bible 156
Chapter XV
    Autumn Ramblings in Northern Michigan 167
Chapter XVI
    Big Heads & Bump Bunkum 175
Chapter XVII
    Shanty Boys of the North Woods 184
Chapter XVIII
    When in Pain - Please Pass the
    Paine's - Hiccup! 194
Chapter XIX
    The Kid From Kalamazoo &
    Other Knights of the Road 204
Chapter XX
    Michigan's Better Angel 217
Chapter XXI
    The Roamer, "America's Smartest Car" 224
Chapter XXII
    A Belated Rebuttal On Russia 233
Chapter XXIII
    Cass County's Crusading Correspondent 239
Chapter XXIV
    Old Bones & Canine Cuisine 249
Chapter XXV
    1837 & 2008: Continuity and Change 260

Sources 267
Index 278

Preface

Exit the expressway onto a two-lane blacktop. Follow the tarmac until it narrows to a gravel lane. Where the road veers north, straight ahead a two-track beckons. Park your vehicle and stride along that winding, sandy portal to the past. And your adventure begins.

Around each meander unknown vistas unfold. Here lies a prairie, rich with columbine, brown-eyed Susans and Queen Anne's lace. At its border stands a row of weathered white pine stumps, jagged roots akimbo, remnants of a pioneer fence. Here towering red pines, planted by CCC youths during the Great Depression, range in long ranks. Here a crumbling fieldstone foundation and nearby clump of lilac bushes mark the place a family called home decades ago.

Distant honking grows louder and louder, and suddenly a great vee of geese wing overhead against the cerulean sky, reenacting an ancient ritual. You chance upon a tall sandy bluff where shanty boys piled their winter's cut and in the spring sent the logs thundering down the rollway to splash into the river and be carried miles downstream to the hungry sawmill.

Here, where the two-track cuts through a bank, the last heavy rain has unearthed a perfect flint arrowhead, knapped centuries before by an Ottawa or Potawatomi brave. Save for that reminder of whose domain this once was, in any direction as far as you can see, no man-made object intrudes. Now let your imagination carry you back to Michigan of long ago….

Welcome to my eleventh volume in the *Voyages Into Michigan's Past* series. Within, I've assembled a cast of some colorful Michigan characters. Ride along with Dr. Osman Goodrich, asleep in the saddle, on his way through the Allegan County wilderness to isolated log cabins. Get to know the Husseys of Battle Creek, intrepid Underground Railroad conductors, and the Agassizs, father and son, Swiss naturalists who made their mark on the

Upper Peninsula. March with little Johnny Clem, the "Drummer Boy of Chickamauga," and Detroit-born Chaplain Corby who absolved the Irish Brigade at Gettysburg.

Celebrate Michigan's first Christmas among the Huron at St. Ignace in 1679, as well as in mid 19th Century villages when Yuletide was just another day of the year. Visit Mackinac Island in the heyday of the fur trade with Harriet Martineau, Anna Jameson and other sophisticated literary ladies. Travel to Ireland of the 1880s with Bishop Borgess, Russia of the 1920s with a young Allegan man named Gerald Dykstra and India during its bloody struggle for independence with Cass County's famed foreign correspondent, Webb Miller.

Enjoy the company of some "strange but true" Michiganders you'll not meet elsewhere: like Albert Whiting who talked to the dead; Samuel Bickley who read the bumps on Flint folks' heads; and Annie Nelles, door knocker and book hawker of the 1860s. And last but not least, hop a fast freight train with Detroit Fatty, Saginaw Slim and the Kalamazoo Kid.

I thank my life partner and muse Priscilla and daughter Maureen for their entering my hen scratchings on yellow legal pads into the computer and daughter Autumn who kept us smiling with her antics. Again, I thank Deborah Neumann for her skilled layout and design of text, illustrations and cover. Thanks also go to Rick and Penny Briscoe, publishers of *Encore* Magazine, where a number of these articles originally appeared, for affording me nine deadlines each year.

I hope you enjoy this book and, maybe, some two-track adventures, as well.

Larry B. Massie
Allegan Forest

I

MICHIGAN'S FIRST CHRISTMAS CELEBRATION

The blare of a trumpet signaled the start of the pageant. Swinging a scepter, the first of the Magi approached from the east. The star of Bethlehem twinkled overhead. A long train of clansmen followed. The second of the Wise Men shouted out, "Why are you journeying." "To see the baby Jesus," the first replied. Whereupon the second Magi and his retinue joined the procession. The third of the Kings of Orient and several hundred of his people did the same.

At the door to the rude, bark-covered chapel, the first of the Magi propped a standard topped with the star. Entering, the three doffed their gaudy feather headdresses, prostrated themselves before the statue of the infant and laid their presents at the foot of the cradle.

It is 1679 near present day St. Ignace at the Straits of Mackinac, and the first recorded celebration of Christmas on Michigan soil has begun. The celebrants are Christianized Huron tribesman speaking in their native Iroquois dialect. The Jesuit priest, Father Jean Enjalran, who orchestrated and observed the proceedings, recorded the event in a report to his superiors in Paris published that year as part of the *Jesuit Relations*, the primary

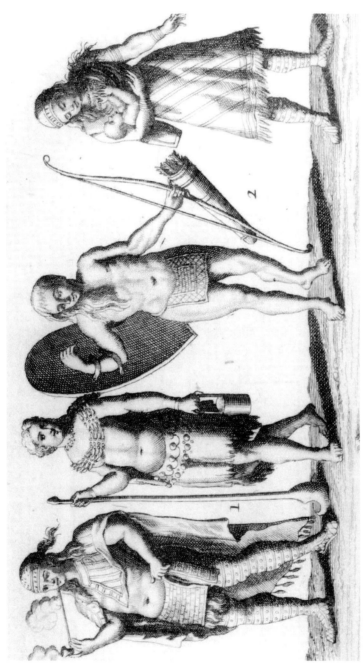

Joseph Lafitau's 1724 book about the Indians of New France contains this fanciful depiction of the Huron people.

source for our knowledge of what transpired during the period of first European contact with the native Americans of the Great Lakes.

Samuel Champlain, "father of New France," had founded Quebec in 1608. He soon developed a burning passion to discover the fabled water route across the continent which would lead to the riches of the orient. In quest of that dream he made his way to Lake Huron in 1615, and, until his death in 1635, he dispatched courageous explorers to the west. Among them, Etienne Brulé and Jean Nicolet first laid eyes on Michigan. In 1615, also, Champlain invited members of the Recollet Order to New France to begin the monumental task of Christianizing the native Americans. Ten years later, the first of the Jesuits joined them, and over the succeeding century those hardy, black-robed priests would carry the cross into the wilderness. Some would become martyrs for their faith.

A Jesuit destined to be immortalized on the Michigan map, Father Jacques Marquette, arrived in New France in 1666. He served at the missions of Sault Ste. Marie, Madeline Island and Mackinac Island. When Mackinac Island's thin soil proved unsuitable for raising corn, he established a mission at nearby Saint Ignace in 1671. There, he and his Huron and Ottawa followers erected a chapel and palisaded fort.

In 1673, Marquette and a young voyageur named Louis Joliet pushed off in a canoe from St. Ignace for an exploratory tour that would take them hundreds of miles down the Mississippi River. Marquette would never again see his beloved mission at St. Ignace. Weakened by dysentery, he died in 1675 and was buried beneath a large wooden cross near the mouth of the river that bears his name. Two years later, a band of Ottawa disinterred his body, scraped the flesh from the bones, as was their tradition, and carried the osseous remains to St. Ignace for burial in the chapel floor.

A 19th century painting of Father Marquette instructing the Indians at St. Ignace.

St. Ignace actually consisted of four district missions catering to the tribes that had fled Canada, Lake Huron and Lake Superior in the face of the onslaught by their ancient rivals, the fierce Iroquois Confederacy. Father Pierre Bailloquet had charge of the mission adjacent the Nippissing and Huron villages. Fathers Henri Nouvel and Jean Enjalran labored at the mission serving 300 Hurons of a different clan and a separate village of some 1,300 Ottawas. In his *Relation of 1679* Enjalran described what other events happened during Michigan's first Christmas celebration.

The Christianized Indians had beseeched the fathers to help them celebrate the holiday in an appropriate fashion, sending children to help construct a "grotto" or crèche. Enjalran wrote touchingly of one little girl who "having brought with care a beautiful sort of grass, said that she had done it in the thought and hope that the little infant Jesus might be laid upon that grass." Once constructed, the crèche "was incessantly visited." As a further testament of their devotion, the Hurons pleaded that the statue of the infant might come to their village.

The ceremony was held on the 12th day of Christmas, Epiphany, marking the visit by the three Magi. Instead of camels treading the desert sands, moccasins crunched across the snow and ice covered St. Ignace fields. In place of gold, frankincense and myrrh, the Huron wise men laid before the cradle strings of the bright porcelain beads they greatly valued. Father Enjalran cradled in his arms the statue of the infant wrapped in a fine linen cloth and, preceded by two French voyageurs bearing a large standard "on which was represented the infant Jesus and his holy mother," advanced solemnly toward the Huron village.

The throng of Indians followed, "chanting the litanies of the virgin" which the Jesuits had taught them. After holding service in the village, the priest carefully returned the statue to the cradle. Whereupon the Indians continued the celebration in their own manner. The Huron

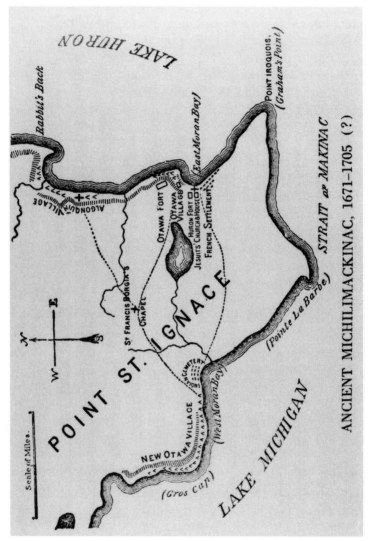

The layout of the various villages and mission at St. Ignace.

prepared a feast for the Ottawa, at which they themselves did not eat as was their custom. The Ottawa then served a special feast for all to enjoy, including the non-Christian tribesmen.

In honor of the visit of the infant Jesus to their village, the Huron staged a ceremonial dance. Only women, who in the Huron culture wielded a great deal of power (they, for example, by their sole vote elected chiefs) performed the dance. Enjalran described the ceremony:

> *The women ranged themselves in two parallel lines at the two sides of a cabin, having in their hands a kind of castanet. Those who are officers commence the song and dance; they have some words to which they apply one of their airs, and these form the refrain of their song which everyone is to repeat in the same air. While the one who has begun goes on with her song agreeably to the words which have served her refrain, - very often, however, varying the air, - she runs and bustles about between these two ranks in a singular manner. In this there is nothing, as formerly (before their Christianization), to violate decency, especially on occasions in which they claim to honor God. Meanwhile the others - repeating at certain intervals the words which form the refrain, and which explain the intention of the one who is dancing - sound their castanets, and move sometimes one foot, sometimes the other, to certain measures without leaving their places. When some word that pleases them occurs in the song they redouble the noise of their castanets, and their cries of joy. Each does, in her term, the same as the first; and it is required of each that she have a special refrain and song.*

Reluctant to end their joyous celebration, the Indians continued the holiday during the following week. On Sunday, a procession of Huron marched along the frozen water of the Straits holding high a standard emblazoned with "the Virgin mother carrying her divine son" to the Ottawa village. The Ottawa received them on the lake shore, and "chanting the litanies of the virgin" they proceeded to the bark-covered chapel where the missionaries had set-up another crèche. Then they enjoyed a feast prepared by the Ottawa during which an Ottawa chief "declared in a harangue that, by that feast, they all united as brothers to obey Jesus, and to entreat the divine child to preserve their children."

The Jesuits found the story of the Nativity particularly appealing to the Indians of the Upper Great Lakes, perhaps because, as many early chroniclers observed, they doted on children. The usually stoic Indians exhibited great affection for all the youngsters of the village.

The Good Friday commemoration of the crucifixion of Christ posed a greater hurdle. It seems their ancient enemies to the west, the dreaded Sioux, tortured captives to a slow and horrible death while stretched out on a cross. The erection of big peeled log crucifixes near each bark-covered chapel gave villagers, many who had lost relatives to the Sioux, qualms about the actual agenda of the missionaries' endeavor.

Be that as it may, the black robes persevered and, according to the *Relations*, found St. Ignace a fertile field for their teachings, baptizing scores each season.

Alas, the acceptance of the Catholic faith could do little to protect the Huron from their fate on earth. Although they spoke an Iroquoian tongue, a feud had raged between the Huron and the tribes of the Iroquois Confederacy to the southeast since prehistoric times. By the mid seventeenth century the Iroquois had acquired firearms from Dutch and later British traders, while the Huron had none. This European technology allowed the

Lafitau's 1724 book pictured a Huron dance.

Iroquois to decimate their ancient enemies. The Huron, skilled agriculturists who dwelt in palisaded villages throughout northern Ontario and who once numbered an estimated 20,000 souls, were nearly obliterated. Several hundred rag-tag refugees settled at St. Ignace.

To protect the fur traders entering the Upper Great Lakes in increasing numbers, the French erected Fort de Buade at St. Ignace during the last decade of the Seventeenth Century. Antoine de la Mothe Cadillac, commandant there from 1694-1701, quarreled with the resident Jesuits missionaries, chiefly over his persistence in supplying liquor to the Indians. In 1701 he removed the garrison to what became Detroit, where the French constructed Fort Pontchartrain.

The resident Indians at St. Ignace drifted away, and the last of the Jesuits left in 1706. A few hundred remnants of the Huron settled around Detroit and in

A typical bark covered chapel as constructed by the Jesuits has been rebuilt at the foot of Fort Mackinac on Mackinac Island.

northern Ohio. They became known as the Wyandotte, a corruption of what they originally called their once mighty nation, the Wendat.

In 1842, most Wyandottes began yet another "trail of tears," removed by the federal government from their dearly loved Great Lakes country to the treeless, dry prairies of Wyandotte County, Kansas. In 1867 after white settlers found that domain attractive, the Wyandottes were moved once again, shunted to a small reservation in the northeast corner of Oklahoma.■

II

THE MOORE-HASCALL DREAM MACHINE

It all started with a dream. Within the little pioneer log cabin on Genesee Prairie in what would become Kalamazoo County's Oshtemo Township, the straw-filled tick stretched across the ponderous rope bed crackled throughout the night as Mary Hascall thrashed and twitched in her sleep. Husband John had inspired her dream the day before with talk of the riches that awaited someone who could figure out a way to efficiently harvest grain from the vast, fertile, flat and treeless terrain known as Prairie Ronde in Schoolcraft and Prairie Ronde townships.

In 1830 the Hascalls had fled Genesee County, New York, over some political troubles in which John had gotten enmeshed. Traveling by Erie Canal boat, Lake Erie steamer and ox-drawn wagon, they made their way to the promising town Titus Bronson had founded and named after himself the year before. Hascall hung out his shingle as a lawyer, but, with frontier legal suits few and far between, he soon left his law books to take up the plow and spade of a farmer.

It was about 1832 that Mary had her dream. The next morning she described her vision of "a large machine going over the prairie drawn by horses and harvesting wheat, and described its motion and appearance." Hascall, of an inventive frame of mind who had earlier conceived the spring balance weighing scales for portable flour-mills, hastened to discuss his wife's dream with Hiram Moore who had emigrated from New

Hiram Moore about 1852.

Hampshire to Climax Prairie in 1831 and who also dabbled as a inventor.

A third pioneer to become involved in the project, Andrew Y. Moore, an unrelated neighbor of Hiram's who went on to become one of the founders of what ultimately became Michigan State University, recalled what ensued: "Hiram asked how he would have it operate. Mr. Hascall replied, holding out his hand with fingers extended, he would run it through the grain, and with the other hand drawn over backwards, he would cut it like that."

In the 1830s the harvesting of grain remained a labor intensive bottle neck that prevented full scale development of the nation's lush agricultural land. Contemporary techniques differed little from those practiced by the ancient Egyptians. Farmers harvested ripe grain with a sickle or the slightly more efficient cradle scythe. Binders laboriously scooped up the cut stalks and tied them into sheaves and at day's end stacked them into shocks that would shed rain. Later the grain was threshed from the straw by beating it with a flail. Many subsequent hours of winnowing separated the chaff from grain. During this period it took an average of 373 man hours of hard labor to produce 100 bushels of wheat.

Suitable weather and optimum ripeness also proved critical factors in grain harvesting. In the 1830s a family with three able laborers dared not plant over 30 acres of wheat. Could Mary Hascall's dream machine provide the breakthrough that would produce an "American agricultural revolution?"

Hiram Moore initially did not intend to become involved in the project - but the dream Hascall had told him about "troubled his mind" for six months until he decided to focus his inventive skills seriously on the venture. By 1834 he had constructed a miniature model which he demonstrated to the personnel of the U. S. Patent Office in Washington. Two years later he and Hascall were jointly granted a patent for their "Improvement in Harvesting Machines for Mowing, Thrashing and Winnowing Grain in One Operation."

Despite the patent, much work remained to perfect the machine. During a trial of the first full-sized combine at Flowerfield Township in 1834, the contraption broke down after 30 feet. According to Andrew Moore, Hiram remarked that day, "I see the shore afar off and it will take a long time to get there, but I will succeed in time."

Hiram Moore continued tinkering with what had become an obsession, ultimately experimenting with five improved versions of the machine. In need of financial backing, Moore convinced Lucius Lyon, land speculater, surveyor, one of Michigan's first senators and a man who repeatedly sought to hit the jackpot through a variety of ill-fated ventures, to invest in the project. Lyon's infusion of funds allowed Moore to order two enhanced machines built in Rochester, New York, in 1837 and shipped to Kalamazoo County the following year. By November, 1839, Lyon could jubilantly report:

> *There is no longer any doubt of the success of the Moore and Hascall harvesting machine. Mr.*

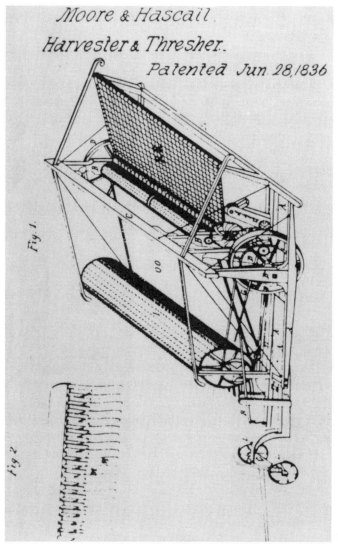

The 1836 patent drawing of the "Harvester & Thresher."

> *Moore has had a machine in the field on Prairie Ronde during the past summer which harvested and threshed 63 acres of wheat in a very superior style and could have harvested 250 acres with greatest ease, at the rate of 20 acres per day....*

A monstrous apparatus, the Moore-Hascall harvester cut a swath 15-feet wide and threshed, cleaned and bagged the grain in one operation. Sixteen horses requiring four drivers pulled the ponderous machine, and three other laborers, including one who tied knots to close the full grain bags, attended the mechanism.

E. Lakin Brown, who had pioneered in Schoolcraft in 1831, saw 600 bushels of his wheat cut, threshed and bagged in one day by the machine. Known as the "Bard of Schoolcraft", Brown later described the harvester in action on Prairie Ronde:

> *But yonder lo! What huge machine?*
> *Drawn by steeds at least sixteen.*
> *Two by two in lengthening line*
> *With even step their strength combine*
> *Four mounted drivers guide their course*
> *And win from each an equal force.*

By the 1840s, the "Mammoth Machine" received widespread publicity. The *Michigan Farmer and Western Agriculturalist* of June 15, 1844, carried an article about the machine's success on Prairie Ronde, describing it as a "noisy, voracious monster, as he clatters along the plain, his flag waving in triumph above, as he crosses the bending heads of wheat with his iron teeth, scatters the straw in seeming wantonness around him and hurls the chaff upwards in clouds while a man stands behind to put out the bags of clean wheat, all ready for the miller."

The *New York Farmer and Mechanic* of October 10, 1844, and the September, 1845, issue of the *Genesee Farmer* of Rochester, New York, printed similar glowing testimonials to the big machine's success. Those accounts, most probably, formed the basis of James Fenimore Cooper's description of the Moore-Hascall machine in his 1848 novel set in Michigan, *Oak*

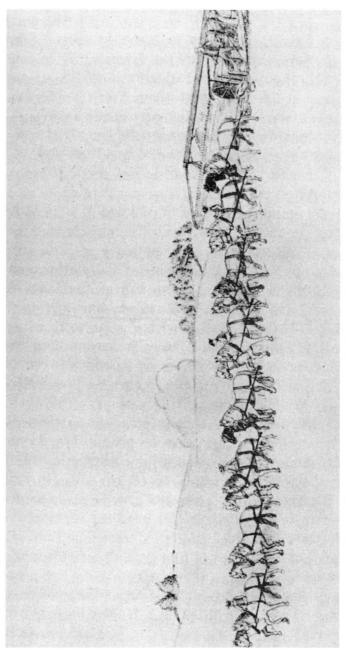

Artist's conception of the combine harvester in operation in Kalamazoo County.

Openings, since he performed little if any on-site research in Kalamazoo County.

Moore continued to experiment with improvements on the harvester. In 1841 he added an angle-edged sickle which could last the entire harvest season without regrinding. That same year Hascall sold his interest in the invention to Lyon for a pittance. Lyon enthusiastically sought additional inventors in order to go into full scale production of the harvester. Unfortunately, Lyon lost most of his fortune through embezzlement by an Iowa land agent, and he reluctantly bailed out of the harvester venture.

Hiram Moore moved to Louisiana in 1845 for health reasons. Having recuperated, he returned to Kalamazoo and represented the county in the State Legislature of 1850. That year Moore and Hascall's original patent expired. Despite petition by Governor Epaphroditus Ransom from Kalamazoo and spirited debate in Congress an attempt to pass a bill to extend the patent failed. Moore immigrated to Wisconsin in 1852 and continued to tinker with his harvester and numerous other inventions until his death in 1875.

In the meantime, A.Y. Moore had built a Moore-Hascall pattern harvester in 1844 and evidently used it successfully for ten seasons near Climax. The final chapter in the harvester saga began in 1854 when Moore shipped his machine from Climax around Cape Horn to San Francisco. His son, Oliver, and a partner herded six champion horses overland. Reunited with the big machine, they threshed 600 acres of wheat that season near Mission San Jose. Unfortunately, the following year an ungreased bearing overheated, and the machine and the wheat field it was in burned up. Oliver Moore made his way back overland to Michigan.

John Hascall died in 1853. Typical of the times, history failed to note the passing of Mary. But, by that time their son, Volney, had begun carving out a notable career in Michigan politics and as a local public benefactor and long time editor of the Kalamazoo *Gazette*.

The Moore Hascall machine focused national attention on Kalamazoo County's agricultural endeavors and won a secure

Andrew Y. Moore, seated in center, and his sons.

niche in history as a prototypical attempt to solve the problems of mechanical harvesting. And while it ultimately failed to enrich its advocates, Mary Hascall's vision had provided quite an exciting ride for a number of them. Which is more than can be said for most dreams. ■

The only known photograph of the Moore-Hascall harvester.

TWO-TRACKS TO MICHIGAN'S PAST

Historical marker installed on a boulder in 1931 on the site of the original Hiram Moore farm near Climax.

III

Dr. Goodrich, Allegan County's Pioneer Physician

With each step the horse raised a little cloud of dust as it plodded along the narrow trail snaking through the Allegan County wilderness. The horse seemed to know where it was going, which was fortunate for the rider slouched forward in the saddle, fast asleep. Like many frontier practitioners, Dr. Osman Dewey Goodrich had learned to take his rest where and when he could get it.

Entering a clearing amidst the forest giants, the horse stopped before a log shanty. The break in riding rhythm woke Goodrich, and he wearily climbed down from the saddle, grasped his little black bag and stumbled toward the cabin door. Early that morning he had received word that an entire family lay sick with fever. Six hours later — during which a physician today might cross the entire continent — he had arrived at his destination, 20 miles away. That was typical of travel in Allegan County in the 1830s.

Goodrich pulled the latchstring and stooped to enter the shanty. As his eyes grew accustomed to the dim light within, he surveyed a pitiful sight. On the only bed in the room lay a man and two or three little ones, bundled high with blankets. They were shaking so hard that the bedstead bounced. Stretched across

Dr. Osman D. Goodrich's likeness appeared in the 1880 Allegan and Barry County History.

the quilts and feather ticks that littered the floor, the mother of the family and four other children lay sweating and panting for breath — burning up with fever. The doctor diagnosed their ailments at a glance — the ague or what we now know as malaria.

Frontier folk had many theories as to what caused the disease; bad water, night air or the so-called poisonous miasma that rose from the rotting vegetation of marshes. But none suspected the clouds of mosquitoes whose bites we now know pass on the disease. One thing was certain, however, rare was the pioneer who did not feel its ravages.

We cannot know for sure exactly how Goodrich treated the family. But chances are he followed the advice given in "Eberle's Practice," since a leather covered, two-volume set bearing his name has survived. Eberle recommended bleeding those experiencing the hot stage of the disease and administering enemas and a "tall dose of opium" to those suffering the chills of the cold stage. For those between stages a solution of powdered

A typical "saddlebag doctor," Charles B. Johnson, attended the University of Michigan Medical School in the 1860s.

"Peruvian Bark," the source of quinine, was recommended. Since Peruvian Bark was apt to be in short supply on the frontier such substitutes as dogwood, tulip poplar or horse-chestnut bark had to suffice. For obstinate cases Eberle suggested remedies ranging from cobweb pills to leeches on the stomach. Happily, and in spite of his medications, Goodrich's patients probably survived since the ague rarely proved fatal.

Born on May 10, 1808, in New Hartford, Oneida County, New York, Goodrich grew up on the farm his pioneer parents had carved out of the wilderness beginning in 1800. At the age of 20, be began studying medicine as an apprentice to a local doctor and in 1834 received his medical degree.

He established his first practice in Huron County, Ohio. Elisa Ely, one of the founders of Allegan, invited him to set up his practice there, and accordingly, in May, 1836, Goodrich hung his shingle in that frontier community. At that time, according to his recollections published in 1880: "there was but one house within 10 miles of Allegan. North and south of the village was an unbroken wilderness, and west, not a dwelling until the shores of Lake Michigan were reached." Soon, however, the sounds of pioneer axes startled the wilderness as homesteaders began carving out farms in isolated settings.

In an era when house calls were the norm, Goodrich spent many long hours "following an Indian trail to the crude home of the early settler who was so unfortunate as to require his service." The hazards of a profession which required him to travel day and night through mosquito-infested swamps, fording streams, encountering wolves and bears, and then sitting up all night with expectant mothers, wore him out. He gave up his practice in 1845 and moved to Connecticut in an effort to regain his health. Ten years later, however, he returned to Allegan, having become converted to a school of medicine known as homeopathy. As opposed to "regular doctors," homeopaths

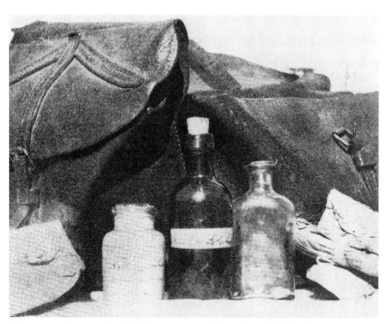

A pioneer physician's saddlebags contained his sole medical aids.

A 19th century homeopathic medicine kit as would have been used by Dr. Goodrich.

prescribed minute doses of drugs that produced effects similar to the patient's complaint. Allopaths recommended drugs that did just the opposite and eclectics let the patient — or next of kin — choose either type of drug. Other practitioners utilized botanic medicines or remedial baths and showers. A few medical "electricians" shocked their patients back to health.

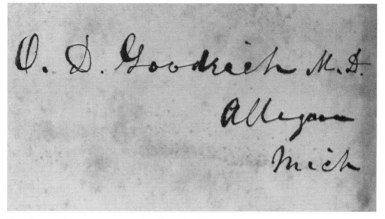

Dr. Goodrich's signature on the flyleaf of his medical guide.

Goodrich's son, Dr. Osman E. Goodrich, followed in his father's footsteps, serving as a homeopathic physician in Allegan from 1866 until his retirement in 1878. By that time and until his death in 1887, the elder Goodrich had earned a position of respect as the community's only surviving saddlebag doctor, having "witnessed the transition of the wilderness into a highly prosperous agricultural section and of a hamlet into a busy and enterprising village.■

IV

"THE WILDEST & TENDEREST PIECE OF BEAUTY ON GOD'S EARTH"

Harriet Martineau gazed in excitement from the deck of the *Milwaukee* as the schooner tacked across the Straits of Mackinac en route to the island known to Michigan's native peoples as Michilimackinac. It was the evening of July 4, 1836, and the sophisticated, 34-year-old British literary lady tempered her disappointment at missing the Independence Day festivities at the fort whose whitewashed bulwarks dominated the island's heights with the sights that followed:

> *The island looked enchanting as we approached, as I think it always must, though we had the advantage of seeing it first steeped in the most golden sunshine that ever hallowed lake or shore. The colours were up on all the little vessels in the harbour. The national flag streamed from the garrison. The soldiers thronged the walls of the barracks; half-breed boys were paddling about in their little canoes, in the transparent waters; the half-French, half-Indian population of the place were all abroad in their best. An Indian lodge was*

This lithograph of Mackinac Island as seen from the Straits appeared in Thomas McKenney's 1827 Tour of the Lakes.

on the shore, and a picturesque dark group stood beside it. The cows were coming down the steep green slopes to the milking. Nothing could be more bright and joyous.

Martineau recorded her impressions of Mackinac Island in *Society in America*, published upon her return to England in 1837. That volume and her *Retrospect of Western Travel*, also based on her American experiences, became contemporary best sellers, although her censorious treatment of aspects of frontier culture did little to endear her with American readers. She lavished on Michigan, however, and Mackinac Island, in particular, little but praise for their pristine beauty.

Martineau was but one of a fascinating circle of women writers, including some of the most gifted and popular of their age, who recorded impressions of Michigan in the 1830s and 1840s. A surprisingly large proportion of those travelers found their way to Mackinac Island which, by then, had already become a Mecca for a growing number of Great Lakes tourists. The vivid word pictures they penned offer intimate glimpses into the island's past.

Harriet Martineau in 1850.

Juliette Kinzie in midlife.

One of the earliest descriptions of the island based on actual observations to be recorded in book form by a woman occurs in Juliette Kinzie's *Wau-Bun: The "Early Days" in the Northwest*. Although not published until 1856, the volume contains Kinzie's classic accounts of her life on the Illinois and Wisconsin frontier in 1830-1833, including a narrative of her voyage from Detroit to Green Bay with a stopover at Mackinac Island in 1830.

John Kinzie, Indian agent at Fort Winnebago, located east of present day Portage, Wisconsin, had married Juliette Magill at her home in New Hartford, New York, the previous month. En route to their new home at the fort, the two climbed aboard the *Henry Clay* at Detroit on a dark, rainy evening in September, 1830. The vessel, a state-of-the-art craft, part of the Lake Erie Steamboat Line fleet, splashed northward, weathering a storm off Thunder Bay and docked at the Mackinac Island pier at nine o'clock in the evening of the succeeding day. That evening the Kinzies enjoyed the hospitality of Robert and Elizabeth Stuart.

Stuart, a long time friend of Kinzie, had joined John Jacob Astor's fur trading empire in 1810 and had served as agent of Astor's American Fur Company at Mackinac since 1819.

Juliette Kinzie observed:

> *These were the palmy days of Mackinac. As the headquarters of the American Fur Company and the entre port of the whole North West all the trade in supplies and goods on the one hand, and in furs, and products of the Indian country on the other, was in the hands of the parent establishment or its numerous outposts scattered along Lakes Superior and Michigan, the Mississippi, or through still more distant regions... It was no unusual thing, at this period, to see a hundred or more canoes of Indians at once approaching the island, laden with their articles of traffic; and if to these we add the squadrons of large Mackinac boats constantly arriving from the outposts, with the furs, peltries and buffalo robes collected by the distant traders, some idea may be formed of the extensive operations and important position of the American Fur Company, as well as the vast circle of human beings either immediately or remotely connected with it.*

Following their inspection of the Mission House erected by the Rev. William Ferry and his wife Amanda in 1825 and the newly constructed Mission Church, the Kinzies hastened to finish their tour of the village as their ship was scheduled to leave at 2:00 that afternoon. Juliette took time to note the residence of Madam Laframboise, a wealthy and influential leader of the local Metis community who had continued to operate her husband's fur trading enterprise following his murder in 1807. The Indian Agency House, "with its luxuries of piazza and gardens," she saw sprawled at the foot of the cliff surmounted by the fort and the "collection of rickety, primitive looking buildings," occupied by the officials of the American Fur

George W. Featherstonhaugh's A Canoe Voyage Up the Minnay Sotor, *published in 1847, included this view of the island in 1834.*

Company which Kinzie told his wife he had superintended the construction of when but a mere boy. Following a luncheon with another notable island family and long time friends of Kinzie, Dr. and Mrs. David Mitchell, the newlyweds hurried aboard the *Henry Clay*.

As the ship steamed out of the little harbor, Kinzie enjoyed one final breathtaking view - "the sloping beach with the scattered wigwams, and the canoes drawn up here and there - the irregular, quaint looking houses - the white walls of the fort, and beyond one eminence still more lofty, crowned with the remains of old Fort Holmes." Glancing down into the crystal clear water she saw fish gliding beneath her and objects lying on the sandy bottom perfectly visible in 50-60 feet of water. "I could hardly wonder," Kinzie quipped, "at the enthusiastic lady who exclaimed: 'Oh! I could wish to be drowned in these pure, beautiful waters!'"

In 1830 the appearance of a steamship in the Straits of Mackinac was a rare event. The *Henry Clay* had deviated from its regular Buffalo to Detroit run specifically to carry government officials and others bound for the Indian treaty negotiations at Green Bay. But by the summer of 1836, when Martineau made her visit to the island, a growing fleet of steamers and sailing vessels routinely operated in the northern waters.

Nevertheless, Martineau had almost missed the opportunity of seeing Mackinac Island. Despite a jolting stagecoach ride from Detroit to Chicago along the notoriously abominable Chicago Military Road, she intended to return over an even worse stretch farther to the north, the Territorial Road. But in Chicago, she learned that a severe rainstorm had rendered that road impassable. The *Milwaukee*, scheduled to leave the following day for Detroit, offered an obvious answer to the dilemma. Six days of sailing, including a brief stop at the vessel's namesake port, but recently platted, brought her to Mackinac Island.

There, Martineau learned to her dismay that the captain intended to tarry but three hours while unloading cargo and the passengers would not be allowed ashore. Refusing to accept the

Mackinac Island's famous Arch Rock as depicted ca. 1890.

"dreadful idea that we might be carried away from this paradise, without having set foot on it," Martineau, with the assistance of a fellow passenger referred to only as Mr. D, most probably Michael Dousman, a well-known fur trader and long time resident of the island, hatched a scheme. The fur trader would insist that his cargo of pelts not be unloaded until morning and his workers, he assured Martineau, would do so "with the utmost possible slowness," thus gaining her time for at least a brief look at the island. A friend communicated to the fort commander, Col. George M. Brooks, Martineau's plight and he and his family graciously agreed to rendezvous with her at 5:00 a.m. for a hurried tour of the island. Martineau described the charming ramble she enjoyed beginning at the slope behind the fort:

> *We wound about in a vast shrubbery, with ripe strawberries under foot, wild flowers all around, and scattered, knolls and opening vistas tempting curiosity in every direction. "Now run up," said the commandant, as we arrived at the foot of one of these knolls. I did so, and was almost struck backwards by what I saw. Below me was the Natural Bridge of Mackinac of which I had heard frequent mention. It is a limestone arch, about one hundred and fifty feet high in the center, with a span of fifty feet, one pillar resting on a. rocky projection in the lake, the other on the hill. We viewed it from above, so that the horizon line of the lake fell behind the bridge, and the blue expanse of waters filled the entire arch. Birch and ash grew around the bases of the pillars, and shrubbery tufted the sides and dangled from the bridge. The soft rich hues in which the whole was dressed seemed borrowed from the autumn sky.*

But even that breathtaking view of Arch Rock in its pristine condition paled compared to what she observed from the site of Fort Holmes. It moved her to biblical hyperbole:

> *I can compare it to nothing but to what Noah might have seen, the first bright morning after the deluge. Such a cluster of little paradises rising out of such a congregation of waters, I can hardly fancy to have seen elsewhere. The capacity of the human eye seems here suddenly enlarged, as if it could see to the verge of the watery creation. Blue, level waters appear to expand for thousands of miles in every direction; wholly unlike any aspect of the sea. Cloud shadows, and specks of white vessels, at rare intervals, alone diversify it. Bowery islands rise out of it; bowery promontories stretch down into it; while at one's feet lies the melting beauty which one almost fears will vanish in its softness before one's eyes; the beauty of the shadowy dells and sunny mounds, with browsing cattle, and springing fruit and flowers. Thus and no otherwise, would I fain think did the world emerge from the flood.*

Martineau had just enough time left to enjoy with the colonel a fine breakfast rarely encountered in her frontier travels of "rich cream, new bread and butter, fresh lake trout and a pile of snow-white eggs." Perhaps partly due to such island fare, the place was so healthy, Brooks informed her, that "people who want to die must go somewhere else." But when she asked about the climate, his response hinted that Mackinac Island was not quite as Eden-like as her few short hours there led her to believe. "We have nine months winter, and three months cold weather," he replied.

Martineau bid farewell to her hosts and boarded the *Milwaukee*, whose captain, "looked grave" over the delay his headstrong passenger had cost him, and sailed from the harbor about 9:00 a.m. As the island, crowned with its whitewashed bulwarks, receded she felt delight "at having the possession of its singular imagery for life" mingled with the sorrow of leaving it. She wrote: "I could not have believed how deeply it is to regret a place, after so brief an acquaintance with it."

A portrait of beautiful red-headed Anna Jameson as a teenager.

A year later, in July, 1837, another cultivated British literary lady arrived on Mackinac Island. Anna Jameson, a beautiful Irish red-head, had embarked on a tour to the north country, in part, to escape the torments of an unhappy marriage to a cold-hearted Toronto judge. She enjoyed a pleasant two days voyage from Detroit to the island on the steamer *Thomas Jefferson*. Her distinguished fellow travelers included the Rev. Samuel A. McCoskry, bishop of the Episcopal Diocese of the new state of Michigan, veteran frontier fighter Gen. Hugh Brady and one of Daniel Webster's sons, either Daniel Fletcher or Edward. Hastily deposited on the wharf as the steamer churned out of the harbor, Jameson found the only full fledged hotel there

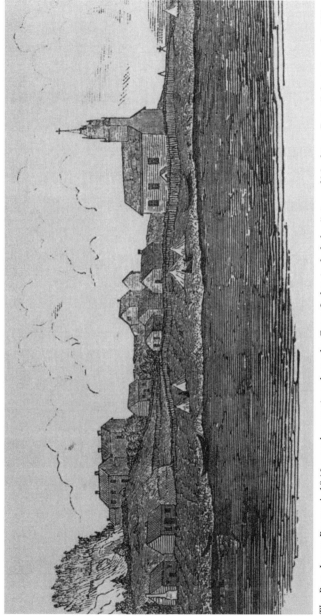

The Rev. James Beaven's 1846 travel narrative about the Great Lakes included a "view of Mackinac Point" depicting the Old Mission Church and nearby Indian lodges.

completely full. Fortunately she was able to secure lodging with resident Indian agent Henry Rowe Schoolcraft and his family. Jameson soon forged a warm friendship with Schoolcraft's half-Chippewa wife, Jane, and later accompanied her on a canoe trip to visit her Indian relatives in Sault Ste. Marie.

During her nearly week long sojourn on the island Jameson enjoyed the usual tourist sites: Arch Rock, Skull Cave, a tour of the fort and a Sunday service in the Old Mission Church. But she found most interesting the hordes of Indians encamped on the beach. These Ottawa, Chippewa, Potawatomi, Winnebago and Menominee families had made their annual pilgrimage to the island to receive treaty payments. She preserved a skillfully crafted word picture of the colorful camp in her travel narrative, *Winter Studies and Summer Rambles in Canada*, published in three volumes in 1838:

> There were more than one hundred wigwams, and round each of these lurked several ill-looking, half-starved, yelping dogs. The women were busied about their children, or making fires and cooking, or pounding Indian corn in a primitive sort of mortar, formed of part of a tree hollowed out, with a heavy rude pestle which they moved up and down as if churning. The dress of the men was very various - the cotton shirt, blue or scarlet coat; were most general; but many had no shirt nor vest, merely the cloth leggings, and a blanket thrown round them as drapery; the faces of several being most grotesquely painted. The dress of the women was more uniform; a cotton shirt, and cloth leggings and moccasins, and a dark blue blanket. Necklaces, silver armlets, silver earrings, and circular plates of silver fastened on the breast, were the usual ornaments of both sexes. There may be a general equality of rank among the Indians; but there is evidently all that inequality of conditions which difference of character and intellect might naturally produce;

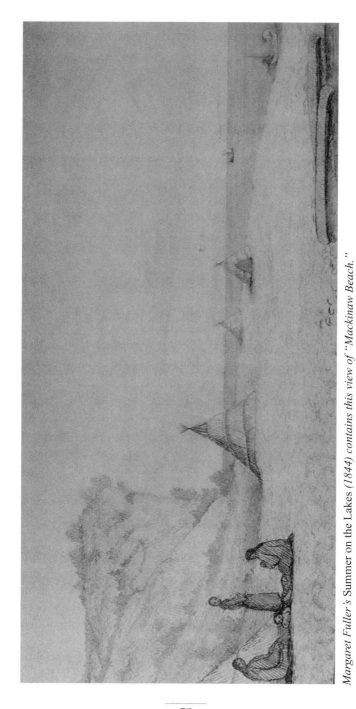

Margaret Fuller's Summer on the Lakes *(1844) contains this view of "Mackinaw Beach."*

there were rich wigwams and poor wigwams; whole families ragged, meager, and squalid, and others gay with dress and ornaments, fat and well-favored.

Jameson grew to appreciate Indian culture. She liked the natives and they liked her, christening her "The Fair English Chieftainess" on Mackinac Island and, following her shooting the Sault Rapids in a birch bark canoe, "Woman of the Bright Foam." The Irish red-head devoted 225 pages of her *Winter Studies* to detailed and sympathetic descriptions of her experiences among the Indians at Mackinac Island and Sault Ste. Marie, their appearance, culture and legends. Those who would recapture this golden era of Mackinac's past are fortunate indeed that such a gifted and sensitive writer spent time there. But because she dared to defy Victorian society's stern mores by traveling unchaperoned to the northern frontier, Jameson received censure from another female writer who visited Mackinac three years later.

Eliza Steele, a prim and proper author of religious books, admonished the female readers of her travel narrative, *A Summer Journey in the West*, against committing errors such as Jameson had to "which the very witchery of her genius would blind you." Warming up to her lecture, Steele sniffed; "However passionate a desire you may entertain for the picturesque, I hope you may never leave the protection of your friends and wander in search of it alone."

Steele had set out from her home in New York City in early June, 1840, for a 4,000 mile summer tour through the Great Lakes, the prairies of Illinois, the rivers Illinois, Mississippi and Ohio and back over the Allegheny Mountains. July 4th found her steamer, the *Constellation*, approaching Mackinac Island, just as the fort's cannon boomed out its mid day salute in honor of the national holiday. Steele enjoyed an afternoon's ramble about the island, viewing Arch Rock, the old French buildings in the village and the fort. She met the fort's commander and Henry Rowe Schoolcraft and family. Steele's impressions of the Indians she encountered differed as radically from Jameson's as did their relative philosophy about "woman's true sphere." Steele wrote:

> *Upon the beach a party of Indians had just landed, and we stood while they took down their blanket sail, and hauled their birch bark canoe, about twenty feet long, upon the shore. These are the Menominees or wild rice eaters, the ugliest Indians I had ever seen - also Winnebagoes, with dark skin, low foreheads and shaggy hair, and have no pretentious to dress.*

Steele thought no better of Indian music than the native's appearance. As the *Constellation* pulled away from the island that afternoon, she observed:

> *Upon the shore sat a group of unearthly beings, one of whom struck several taps upon a sort of drum, accompanied by the others in what sounded like a wolf recitative - at the end of this all united in a yell which died away over the lake, much in the style of a howling blast accompanied by the shrieks of a drowning traveler.*

Sarah Margaret Fuller, who visited Mackinac Island in 1843.

Truly, beauty is in the eye, or the ear, of the beholder. And while prudish Mrs. Steele perceived Mackinac Island's colorful sights and sounds as ugliness and shrieks, others, fortunately, interpreted with more toleration. In August, 1843, for example, Margaret Sarah Fuller arrived for a stay on the island. She encountered nearly 2,000 Indians encamped along the beach and the descriptions she recorded in *Summer on the Lakes* (Boston, 1844) offer a more sympathetic treatment of Indian culture.

One of the most distinguished literary women of her era, a friend of Ralph Waldo Emerson, a member of the transcendentalist circle and editor of that movement's literary journal *The Dial*, a critic for Horace Greeley's New York *Tribune* and a prominent advocate for various reforms including women's rights, Fuller wrote about her Mackinac Island experience with the true eye of an artist. She painted vibrant word pictures of Arch Rock, Sugar Loaf, Fort Mackinac, the view from Fort Holmes and especially the Indians - while deftly inserting her feminist viewpoint:

> *On the other side, along the fair curving beach, below the white houses scattered on the declivity, clustered the Indian lodges, with their amber-brown matting so soft and bright of hue in the late afternoon sun. The first afternoon I was there, looking down from a near height, I felt that I never wished to see a more fascinating picture. It was an hour of the deepest serenity; bright blue and gold, with rich shadows. Every moment the sunlight fell more mellow. The Indians were grouped and scattered among the lodges, the women preparing food, in the kettle or frying pan, over the many small fires, the children, half naked, wild as little goblins, were playing both in and out of the water. Here and there lounged a young girl, with a baby at her back, whose bright eyes glanced, as if born into a world of courage and of joy, instead of ignominious servitude and slow decay. Some girls were cutting wood, a little*

This lithograph of Sugar Loaf Rock appeared in Foster and Whitney's 1851 Report on the Geology of Lake Superior.

from me, talking and laughing in the low musical, tone, so charming in the Indian women. Many bark canoes were upturned upon the beach, and by that light, of almost the same amber as the lodges, others coming in, their square sails set, and with almost arrowy speed, though heavily laden with dusky forms, and all the apparatus of their household. It was a scene of ideal loveliness, and these wild forms adorned it, as looking so much at home in it.

Fuller stayed nine days on the island and spent much of her time with the Indians. From her observations she became convinced that the Indian women occupied "a lower place than women among the nations of European civilization." But while saddened by the wretched state to which many had been reduced by trader's whiskey and missionaries' zeal to eradicate their native culture, she felt that her experiences at Mackinac had acquainted her with the soul of the Indian race and that "there was a greatness, unique and precious, which he who does not feel will never duly appreciate the majesty of nature in this American continent."

Fuller took a jaunt of several days to Sault Ste. Marie, where she emulated Jameson's feat of six years previous and shot the rapids in an Indian canoe. Returning to Mackinac Island for several more days, she watched the Indians departing, not quite as pleasant a sight as their arrival. Furthermore, she noted, "they left behind, on all the shore, the blemishes of their stay, - old rags, dried boughs, fragments of food, the marks of their fires. Nature likes to cover up and gloss over spots and scars, but it would take her some time to restore that beach to the state it was in before they came." So much for the modern stereotype of an Indian observing a littered landscape with a tear trickling down his cheek.

Thus did five diverse women record their varied impressions of Mackinac Island during the golden era when its tourist industry was but in its infancy. A generation would pass before another coterie of women writers fell under the spell of

Arch Rock as seen from the beach, ca. 1890.

the island. In 1870 Constance Fenimore Woolson published the first of many articles, short stories and novels about island life. As the 19th Century drew to a close she was joined in her literary efforts at mining the island's history, legends and romantic beauty by Mary Hartwell Catherwood, Lorena M. Page, Grace Franks Kane and others.

By then, the spectacle of 2,000 Indians camped along the beach had become a thing of the past. But to this day hundreds of thousands of tourists each year continue to enjoy spectacular sunsets and sunrises, climb the steps to Fort Mackinac, sit for a spell in the quaint pews of the Old Mission Church, gaze through Arch Rock, contemplate Sugarloaf, imagine the horror of Alexander Henry awaking in Skull Cave, and savor other of the same attractions that literary ladies marveled at more than century and half ago. And of those who really get to know the island many would agree with Martineau that it remains "the wildest and tenderest piece of beauty that have yet seen on Gods earth."■

This view of Mackinac Island, ca. 1830s, appeared in Robert Sears's Pictorial Description of the United States (1848).

V

TALKING WITH THE DEAD

"Young Albert B. Whiting saw dead people all around him. He was not afraid of them. They were his friends, he talked to them and they communicated back. As a toddler first learning to speak he told his parents about "the people." They scolded him to "hush," there was no one there, "something must be the matter with your eyes or brain."

A sickly youth with a frail, slim body and abnormally large head, Whiting's chances for survival troubled his parents. Several physicians examined the boy and concluded he "would not live to see his 12th year." When the child overheard such prognoses, he grew angry, replying, "I will live, for the people say so." When one celebrated doctor delivered a similar diagnosis in front of Whiting, he exclaimed "I will live to visit your grave, for the man in the gray cloak (one of the people) says so, and he knows."

The strange boy was born December 14, 1835 in East Abington, Mass., the oldest son of Albert and Rachel Whiting. At the age of 12, he contracted a lung ailment, which nearly brought on pneumonia. After many weeks of illness during which the physician's prediction appeared to be born out, Whiting survived. But the severity of that

The portal of the "realm of the dead" as depicted in a spiritualist book of 1853.

ordeal had somehow taken away his ability to see spirits. He recorded in a letter to friends:

> *An indefinable loneliness came over me, and in time I grew to look upon the past second sight as a delusion, pleasant, but gone forever. I thought I saw the correctness of my friends' assertion, - that it was a shadow on the eye or mind, - and I seemed to myself to have grown immeasurably older by its removal... I saw nothing of a spiritual character; I believed death to be an eternal sleep and thought of it only with a shudder.*

As a teenager, Whiting attended the nearby East Bridgewater Academy where, despite repeated bouts of ill health, he excelled, particularly in writing. In the spring of 1853, the family moved to Michigan in hopes that a change of climate would benefit young Whiting's health. They settled on a small farm adjoining the village of Brooklyn, Jackson County, where Michigan's salubrious summer and fall helped bring revitalization to the sickly 17-year-old.

Shortly after Whiting's 18th birthday, "suddenly and without warning, the spirit-sight, the lost gift of his childhood, returned to him." Whiting recorded what happened in his journal:

> *On the night of the 21st of January, 1854, I was suddenly awakened by four persons, bearing the appearance of Indians, who stood before me as distinctly as any persons I ever saw in my life. My room was brilliantly illuminated, although the night was very dark; I rubbed my eyes and half arose, to be sure I was awake; but there they stood. At length one of them - a chief of gigantic stature - approached my bedside and addressed me as follows:*

"Child of earth, take back the inheritance of your ancestors, the gifts of your childhood! We are spirits; we will give you health, and knowledge of spiritual life and intercourse. Other spirits will make you an instrument in their hands to proclaim this knowledge to the world. Tell what you have seen."

Then the Indians were gone and the room in darkness again. Suddenly an ancient wooden clock struck twelve - three times in succession.

Expecting ridicule, Whiting told no one of his experience. The Indians returned night after night,

Albert B. Whiting as he looked just before his passing to the spirit land.

enjoining him to announce to the living world the existence of the spirit realm. Finally on the tenth such night, fearing that perhaps he had become insane, Whiting cried out in anger, "If you are spirits, why can't you bring someone whom I will know, instead of Indians altogether."

The next night Whiting's beloved little brother, who had died of illness ten years before, appeared before him, saying, "It is indeed true that spirits exist and communicate. It is my pleasure to return, giving my testimony to sustain what has been told you. I live, and am happy; your brother still in love, truth and reality."

Still Whiting could not make up his mind to "come out" and risk being branded a madman. Other episodes persisted. He saw an Indian standing along the road who vanished, laughing, as Whiting approached. A strange, silent, old bearded man appeared in his room one day. When Whiting described him to his father, he replied, "That is your grandfather Whiting - my father." Whiting had never seen his grandfather, and no portrait existed.

The Indian spirits continued to haunt his nights, throwing him into a "semi-conscious trance," and they put him through various exercises to improve his health. Once the chief had him rowing a boat up and down the nearby River Raisin. Awaking the next morning, he rubbed his eyes and thought what an odd dream he had had. Then reaching into his pocket, he found a still-wet water lily he remembered picking in his "dream."

Other spirits began controlling him at times, causing him to speak in their voices, to sing, to write, sometimes with both hands at once and reversed so that it was unreadable unless held before a mirror. Then came the telekinesis, as he was lifted into the air and moved about without his control. Once, in the presence of his mother and sister, he sailed through the air 35-feet from one lounge to land safety on another in a different room of the house.

As might be expected, news of these remarkable feats spread, drawing crowds of curious visitors. Many departed, convinced of the possibility of communicating with the spirit world.

The belief that spirits survive physical death and can influence the living runs as a common thread through numerous primitive religions. The history of Christianity is also punctuated with episodes of witch mania, poltergeists, demonic possession and exorcism. The mass religious movement known as modern American spiritualism began in 1848 through the agency of teen- aged sisters, Margaretta and Catherine Fox.

Several months after the Fox family had moved into a small frame cottage in the village of Hydesville, New York, they began experiencing mysterious footsteps and rappings, unexplained movement of objects, unseen touches and other occult occurrences. The Fox sisters experimented and discovered they could communicate with the invisible noise-maker, the spirit of a murdered peddler, who rapped out answers to their questions. When neighbors gathered to witness the phenomenon, he knocked for them as well.

The Foxes took to the stage as mediums in nearby Rochester and soon the "Rochester Rappers" inspired others to take up the new religion that proved "there is no death." A spiritualistic epidemic swept the country with western New York and Michigan, which had been settled by pioneers from that region, becoming epicenters. Scores of converts penned ghostly tracts while under the influence of the hereafter and many others discovered they had powers of occult dialogue. Soon Ouija boards, spirit slate writing, table tippings and séances enriched American popular culture.

About six months after Whiting's initial contact with the Indian spirits (whom many other mediums also claimed as their guides from the hereafter), he experienced his first "contact" by Giovani Farini, the spirit

The house in Hydesville, N.Y., where the Fox sisters launched modern American spiritualism in 1848.

of a 17th century Italian poet and Catholic cardinal, and he found himself speaking and singing in Italian. Farini finally convinced him of his destiny, and Whiting launched a stage career, delivering stirring spiritualist spiels and demonstrations of his ability as a medium throughout Michigan, first to Albion, Marengo, Marshall, Ceresco, Battle Creek and then Livonia and Detroit and, with growing popularity, ultimately across the eastern and midwestern states. During his travels, Farini watched over him like a guardian angel. In July, 1856, Whiting attempted to board the steamer *Northern Indiana* bound from Buffalo to Toledo. Farini took him by the arm and ordered him to take another steamer to Detroit. En route the *Northern Indiana* caught fire with a loss of 50 lives.

Eighteen sixty proved a banner year for Whiting. He published a 100-page pamphlet, "Religion and Mortality," which enjoyed considerable sales at his public appearances. Whiting moved with his mother and sister to Albion that year, and he set up a side business as co-proprietor of a shoe store. It may have been the rhythmic tapping of the shoemaker's hammer that inspired him to begin composing songs and music about that time, mostly of a spiritualist theme. He commissioned the Blakeman & Gibbs melodeon factory at the corner of Kalamazoo's Rose and Main Streets to construct one of its award-winning, magnificent, rosewood instruments (a type of keyboard organ) on which he plinked out his compositions. Whiting's *Land of the So Called Dead* became a minor hit.

But the most important event of 1860 was the beginning of a relationship with yet another "spirit guide," a 12th century Persian Magi who, because of his utterly unpronounceable name, preferred to be called simply, "The Old man." In addition to augmenting Whiting's repertoire with eastern magic, the Old Man also watched over him. In 1861 while in Chicago, he tripped and plunged down the steep stone steps of the railroad depot. The Old Man caught him, and he received only a slight bruise. Onlookers gasped at his walking away from what should have been a bone-breaking plummet.

It was about that time, also, that Whiting made a pilgrimage to the grave of the doctor who said he wouldn't live to see 12.

In addition to his spiritualism beliefs, Whiting became a free-thinker in other matters. He earned a

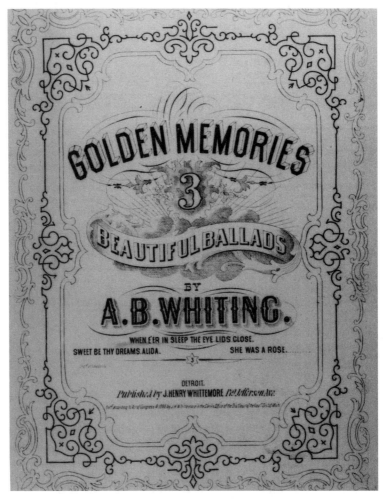

An example of A. B. Whiting's spiritualism songs published in Detroit in 1866.

reputation as a "copperhead" during the Civil War because of his advocacy of peace with the South. He also voiced objections to a proposed new Michigan constitution in 1868 because its articles seemed intolerant of any religion except organized Christianity.

Whiting's hectic schedule and incessant traveling helped bring on a return of his old health problems. He continued to lecture despite a severe throat condition which prevented him from swallowing anything but liquids. He sought the service of a clairvoyant physician in Milford, Mrs. McCain. While under her care, and perhaps because of it, Whiting joined the spirit realm on September 4, 1871, at the age of 36. "A large concourse of people, of all shades of belief and opinion religiously" attended Whiting's Albion funeral. A choir singing *Land of the So Called Dead* accompanied by somber strains of the glorious Kalamazoo melodeon consoled the mourners.

In 1872 Whiting's sister, R. Augusta Whiting, published a biography of her beloved brother, incorporating many of his letters, journal entries and poems. It went through at least two editions, avidly read by thousands of Michiganders who rejected traditional religion in favor of belief in communications with the departed. In the 20th century, spiritualism would be embraced by best-selling novelist Stewart Edward White from Grand Rapids, Arthur Conan Doyle, of Sherlock Holmes fame, and other literati. Curiously, the tattered copy of Whiting's biography before me bears a faint ghostly inscription on the first free endpaper in handwriting very similar to that of Whiting's autograph printed on the frontispiece below his portrait: "Mary Sherman. With remembrance of the Subject." ■

VI

SCIENTISTS IN THE NORTH COUNTRY

In a cultivated French accent, Professor Louis Agassiz launched his lecture. Before him lay a quantity of fish, specimens of the various species netted from the St. Marys Rapids that boiled and roared in the background. "Poisson" he mumbled in his enthusiasm, while temporarily lapsing into his native tongue. Warming to his subject, the professor intoned:

> *The gar-pike is the only living representative of a family of fishes which were the only ones existing during the deposition of the coal and other ancient deposits. At present it occurs only in the United States.*

It was a June day in 1848, and the coterie of students and other scientists who had accompanied Agassiz on his exploratory tour of Lake Superior listened in awe to his learned discourse. He continued:

> *The white-fish has all the characters of the salmons, but no teeth. Among those I obtained today, is a new species, characterized by a smaller mouth and more rounded jaw. To the same family belongs the lake 'herring,' which is no herring at all. This species has a projecting lower jaw and is undescribed... Here is a little fish which on*

> *hasty examination would seem to belong to the salmon... but it is a new genus. Fossil fishes of this family occur in great numbers in the cretaceous period; they are the first of the osseous fishes.*

During the two months spent in the North Country, Agassiz's scintillating lectures about fish, birds, geology or whatever else was encountered during the day's explorations became a welcome part of his retinue's routine, and the thick volume he would co-author stands as a classic, the first scientific account of the natural history wonders of the Lake Superior region. Agassiz's work would influence Charles Darwin and other leading scientists of the era.

Born in one of the French cantons of Switzerland in 1807, the son of a Protestant minister and a physician's daughter, as a youth Agassiz developed an insatiable interest in natural history,

Louis Agassiz at the age of 55.

fishes in particular. He earned a medical degree in Munich in 1829 and a Ph.D. the following year. In Paris in 1831 he first met the barons Alexander von Humbolt and Georges Cuvier, two of the leading naturalists of the era. Agassiz became Cuvier's devoted disciple and subsequently adopted his inflexible antagonism to the evolutionary theory that would be first fully articulated by Darwin in 1859. That unfortunate alignment, in conjunction with his deeply pious religious views, prevented him from reaching the pinnacle of success which his many natural history publications might have brought. Nevertheless, his work continues to command respect.

    A turning point in Agassiz's career came in 1846 when he arrived in America to deliver a series of lectures, and he decided to remain. He spent much of 1847 on a coast survey ship cruising the shores of Massachusetts while studying marine life. On June 15, 1848, Agassiz and seventeen of his students and other scientists set out for their tour of Lake Superior. One of the students, James Elliot Cabot, wrote a running commentary on their travels which appeared in Agassiz's book *Lake Superior*, published in 1850.

    After boarding a steamer at Buffalo, 80-hours of travel brought the party the 663 miles to Mackinac Island where they found they had just missed the weekly ship to Sault Ste. Marie. Cabot described the village which had already emerged as a leading tourist Mecca of the north:

> *We landed on the little wooden wharf in face of a row of shabby cabins and stores, with "Indian curiosities" posted up in large letters to attract the steamboat passengers during the brief stop for fish. Over their roofs appeared the whitewashed buildings of the Fort stretching along the ridge. The inhabitants of the place, looking down on us from all sides, as from the lower benches of a theatre, soon perceived that we had not departed with the steamer, and we were soon plied with invitations to the two principle lodging houses.*

An 1855 wood cut of the village and fort at Mackinac Island.

Despite periodic rain showers, the tourists took in the sights which continue to attract summer hordes, Arch Rock, Sugar Loaf and Fort Mackinac. Fudge evidently had yet to take its honored place. Cabot, who had visited the island before, remembered finding a fragment of human skull on the floor of the little cave where Alexander Henry hid after the massacre at Fort Michilimackinac, thus attesting to the correctness of Henry's narrative about "Skull Cave."

Agassiz went fishing in the rain and then with scalpel in hand before a table covered with "fishes little and big" regaled his students with another lengthy lecture on piscine anatomy. The following morning, rather than wait a week for the next steamer, Agassiz decided to hire a Mackinaw boat and some voyageurs to reach the Sault. Cabot described the craft as a "cross between a dory and a mud-scow, having something of the shape of the former and the clumsiness of the latter."

After stopping for lunch on Goose Island, by twilight the party prepared to camp for the night on a small rocky island, probably one of the Les Cheneaux. A group of the scientists insisted on being landed on a sandy beach bordered by underbrush on the mainland to hunt for beetles, despite the voyageurs' warning that they would be devoured by "les mouches." Sure enough, no sooner had the others landed on the rocky island and lit a campfire "when cries were heard from the main land, and on looking around we saw our friends, some with their heads bound up in handkerchiefs, other beating the air with branches; all vociferating to us to 'Send the boat,' and on the whole, manifesting the most unmistakable symptoms of mosquitoes." During much of their journey similar encounters with mosquitoes and black flies would render camping along the shores of lakes Huron and Superior considerably less than delightful.

The next morning, off at 4:30, the travelers passed the lighthouse at De Tour constructed the year before and stopped for breakfast at a settlement of "lime-burners" on Lime Island. There they found a tavern and enjoyed tea with maple-sugar and "bread of the place, somewhat like sweetened plaster-of-Paris." Passing the British-owned St. Joseph Island, the party noted the

The title page of Agassiz's Lake Superior *featured a vignette of the scientists en route.*

ruins of old Fort St. Joseph which had been burned by the Americans during the War of 1812. Canoeing up the shallow mud flats of Mud Lake, (Munuscong Lake) the scientists reached Sault Ste. Marie on the evening of June 26th where they found accommodations in the St. Marys Hotel.

Cabot penned a picturesque description of Sault Ste Marie, the oldest settlement in Michigan, founded as a mission by Father Marquette in 1668:

> *The most striking feature of the place is the number of dram-shops and bowling alleys. Standing in front of one of the hotels I counted seven buildings where liquor was sold, besides the larger "stores" where this was only one article among others. The roar of the bowling alleys and the click of billiard balls are heard from morning until late at night. The whole aspect is that of a western village on a fourth of July afternoon. Nobody seems to be at home, but all out on a spree, or going a fishing or bowling. There are no symptoms of agriculture or manufactures; traders enough, but they are chatting at their doors or walking about from one shop to another. The wide platforms in front of the two large taverns are occupied by leisurely people, with their chairs tilted. Nobody is busy, but the barkeepers, and no one seems to know what he is going to do next.*

Cabot explained the wild and woolly state of affairs at the Sault, in some respects unchanged to this day, as the result of the ease in which cheap liquor could be smuggled from Canada and the fact that many of the inhabitants found employment irregular, with wages earned in lump sums and "seasons of labor followed by intervals of idleness." Contrary to the present, he described the Canadian Sault as "a thin straggling village" not as the major metropolis of the two Saults linked by the International Bridge.

On June 30, the explorers conveyed their luggage, equipment and supplies over the swampy, nearly mile long,

A view of Water Street, Sault Ste. Marie, in 1850. The St. Marys Hotel, where the scientists stayed, is seen on the right forefront of the street.

portage beside the rapids. The first Sault Canal which would make possible the profitable extraction of the Upper Peninsula's mineral riches, would not open until 1855. In two canoes and a large Mackinaw boat propelled by a dozen voyageurs, the explorers were off on their adventurous six weeks on Lake Superior. Agassiz led the way in his canoe with a big cast iron frying pan lashed to the prow as a figurehead.

After paddling between Gros Cap and Point Iroquois, "the Pillars of Hercules of Lake Superior," unfortunately for the Michigan narrative possibilities, Agassiz chose to travel along the northern shore of the big lake. On August 15th they were back at the Sault electing to shoot the legendary Sault Rapids. Cabot described that feat, dared only by voyageurs and native Chippewa skilled in the dangerous descent: "It was startling in looking down over the side to see the boulders on the bottom twitched by so quickly it was impossible to see their forms. It was like looking down from a railway car upon the sleepers"

In addition to Cabot's narrative, Agassiz's book included detailed description of Lake Superior vegetation, mammals, beetles, butterflies, shells, fish, fossils, reptiles, birds, meteorology and geology. Despite his lifelong antagonism toward Darwin's theory of evolution, Agassiz sent him an inscribed copy of Lake Superior in 1850. Darwin wrote back in thanks commenting, "I have begun to read it with uncommon interest, which I see will increase as I go on."

Agassiz continued his nature explorations until his death in 1873. His many books recount travels over much of the United States, South America and the Pacific coast. Many of his scientific studies, including works on glaciation and fossils, remain classics. By his first marriage he fathered a son, Alexander, who became a distinguished scientist in his own right. Alexander Agassiz also made a valuable contribution to the development of mining ventures in the Upper Peninsula. But that is another story to be told in Chapter 12. ∎

The scientists encamped along the shore of Lake Superior in 1848.

VII

WHEN CHRISTMAS WAS JUST ANOTHER DAY

December 25, 1855, proved a busy day for George DeLano a farmer in Kalamazoo County's Cooper Township. As recorded in his diary, first he had his team of horses shod at Packards, a local blacksmith. Then he mended his bobsled and heaped it high with firewood to sell in Kalamazoo. On December 25th of the following year he carried hams to his brother Ephraim to smoke and hauled wood out of the forest for Kalamazoo. He varied his work routine with a social visit to a neighbor in the evening. The highlight of December 25, 1857, was his attendance at a temperance lecture. His diary entry for 1858's December 25th noted he "went to Woodards to see about my taxes in the a.m. in the p.m. done chores."

Horse shoeing and splitting wood, chores, taxes and lectures on the evils of alcohol - what about visions of sugar plums and jolly old elves, stockings hung by the chimney with care, Christmas trees and carolers, mistletoe and eggnog? What about Christmas?

Based on an examination of hundreds of 19th Century diary entries penned by southwestern Michiganders, found among the holdings of the Archives and Regional History Collection at Western Michigan

In this ca. 1910 postcard Santa brings both presents and the Christmas tree.

University, Delano's activities on Christmas were pretty much the norm for the time. Despite popular beliefs to the contrary, for many Michigan men, women and children antebellum Christmas was simply another day of work, with post offices, stores and other commercial establishments engaged in "business as usual."

Stephen Van Rensellar Earl, a neighboring Cooper Township farmer recorded in his diary that on December 24, 1860, he went to Cooper and got a gallon of vinegar of Lillie Smith. The next day he "chopped wood in the forenoon and at noon helped about the chores." Christmas of 1861 found him sleighing to Cooper where he mailed a letter. Then he "came home and chored around until night and stayed at home." On Christmas 1862 he recorded: "A warm and cloudy morning. Sandford came home and we moved some fence and fixed the barnyard. In the afternoon I went to the store. I went to Otsego and attended the installation of the officers of the lodge." On Christmas of the following year Earl and his son Charley "went over to Rouse's sawmill to see that work."

Washington A. Engle of Hartford, who in 1856 was a medical student at the University of Michigan, spent Christmas eve of that year attending lectures by Prof. Denton on dyspepsia and Prof. Ford on the stomach. On Christmas day he and a fellow student "sat for our likenesses for which we pay $1.25."

Even some men of the cloth, for whom Christ's birthday ought to have had special significance, failed to mention the event in their diaries. Benjamin Farley, a preacher from Burr Oak in St. Joseph County, for example, recorded on December 25, 1837, "At Home - hauled wood and regulated things. Brother Adams came here." On Christmas Day three years later his sole entry was, "went to Mr. Thralls on a visit." The following year's Christmas he wrote, "at home - not very well - pleasant weather."

A few diarists mention it being Christmas day, but only in passing. In 1855 George Reynolds of Berrien

As late as 1910 Santa's appearance had not been standardized. It took Coca-Cola advertisements from the 1920's & 1930's to do that.

Springs wrote, "Christmas day and pretty cold - not as cold as yesterday - snowed all day - very heavy several times." The next year he again noted it was Christmas and that "I have been sawing wood all day." In 1857 he wrote, "been at work all day." Christmas of 1862 brought unseasonably warm weather. Reynolds recorded, "I was sawing wood and sweat like summer."

One explanation for such wholesale disregard for a holiday that has evolved into the festive and fiscal highlight of the calendar lies with the geographic origins of the majority of the pioneers who streamed into Michigan in the late 1820s and 1830s. The story of the numerous DeLano clan, which took up pioneer homesteads in Kalamazoo and Allegan counties, was typical of the times. Following the War of 1812, elements of the family began migrating westward. From Massachusetts some shifted to the Albany, New York, region and others settled farther west in Wayne and Orleans County, New York. By the 1830s it was time for the next generations to seek their fortunes in "Michigania."

The many of settlers from New England brought Michigan positive advantages - the Puritan work ethic and faith in a strong school system, for example. But Puritans had long abhorred festive celebrations of Christ's birthday which they considered of a pagan nature. Following the Puritan ascendancy in England in 1742, Parliament decreed that on the day "commonly known as Christmas, no observance shall be had, nor any solemnity used or exercised in churches in respect thereof." Even plum puddings and mince pies were outlawed as heathen customs.

When the restoration of King Charles II ended the repressive Puritan commonwealth, Christmas returned to England, gradually evolving into the holiday immortalized by Charles Dicken's *A Christmas Carol*. But in New England the Puritan code remained firmly in place. The General Court of Massachusetts, for example, enacted a law making any observance of December 25th a penal offense in 1659. That law was ultimately repealed, but the Puritan aversion to Christmas prevailed. Those who ventured to celebrate might look to the example of the Hessian troops whom Washington crossed the Delaware and surprised while engaged in drunken Christmas revelry. Not until 1856 would Massachusetts finally declare Christmas a legal holiday.

While Christmas remained largely taboo in New England, other sections of the country developed well defined traditions. The holiday was joyously celebrated in the South through the importation of European customs such as gift giving, caroling, the Yule log, decorative greenery and fireworks. The Germans in Pennsylvania and elsewhere brought to the New World such cherished traditions as Christmas trees and St. Nicholas. And while New Englanders were originally dominant in Michigan, other immigrants who hailed from regions where Christmas was celebrated or whose families cherished holiday pleasures transplanted their various traditions to the peninsulas.

Levi and Eveline Lawrence lived in western New York prior to pioneering Little Prarie Ronde, Volinia Township, Cass County, in the 1830s. As a child Levi had spent some time with his father in the Owenite community at New Harmony, Indiana. The Lawrences also belonged to the Swedenborgian Church - in short, they appear to have been freethinkers. Their inclinations to "march to the sound of a different drummer" included Christmas celebrations. Eveline noted in her diary that on December 24, 1856, she "arranged the Christmas gifts for the boys just as loving hearts used to do for me years ago." The following year's Christmas she was suffering a case of the "blues." She wrote: "At night arranged the Christmas gifts for Pa and the boys and went to bed feeling quite depressed thinking of the merry Christmas at home and almost wishing I were a child again with

This ca. 1905 Santa with a brown coat coasted down to lucky households.

someone to love me." Happily the morning's festivities put her in a better mood. She wrote, "We all had a merry time. I was much surprised to find a silk dress in my stocking" (and who wouldn't be).

The decade of the 1860s marks a dramatic change in the typical Michigan family's observance of Christmas. Gradually most of the diaries examined began to reflect a growing acceptance of the Christmas spirit. Why so is open to conjecture. Perhaps Civil War soldiers wrote home about how the holiday was celebrated in other sections of the country, especially the South. Perhaps the mass arrival in the 1840s of immigrants from Germany, Holland and other European nations with long standing Christmas traditions helped popularize the concept. Then too, the availability of nationally circulated magazines such as *Godies Ladies Book*, which pictured Queen Victoria's Christmas tree in the early 1840s, increasingly promoted the holiday via seasonal stories and colorful advertising. For whatever the reason, Christmas trees, holiday celebrations, turkey dinners and gift-giving appear with greater frequency in diaries of the 1860s.

George DeLano first mentioned the holiday in his diary for 1861. On the 25th of December he wrote: "Father, Joel and Mary with us for a Christmas gathering." Four years later he recorded: "Edwin and Adaline came home and we had a Christmas chicken pie." By Christmas Eve 1868 he had heartily embraced the spirit: "In the evening at the church to see the gifts taken from the Christmas tree - received a box of tobacco of the first quality." The next day he "went to Edwins, a Christmas gathering, a very pleasant time."

DeLano's Cooper Township neighbor Stephan V. Earl showed no sign of accepting Christmas in his diaries until 1869 when he noted on December 24th: "In the evening we went over to Philetus Day's to have a sing preparing for the tree tomorrow evening." The next day: "after

Fittingly for Michigan's developing automobile industry this ca. 1908 "Daddy X-mas" arrived by bus.

doing up our chores, Edna went to the husking and Nancy and I went out to the schoolhouse and helped to prepare the Christmas tree and put on the presents - came home and did up the chores and then took the folks and our organ to the schoolhouse and attended the meeting in the evening and had a very fair time."

The "chores" that appear in nearly all diary entries were an integral and unavoidable aspect of life on the Michigan farm. Sally Haner of rural St. Joseph County near Three Rivers recorded her domestic activities during Christmas. On December 24, 1864, she "helped Mary all day - she baked 15 pies and a pan of fried cakes." The following year's Christmas day fell on a Monday - the traditional wash day more sacred than even the holiday. So Haner spent Christmas morning amid big copper boilers and scrub boards. On December 24, 1869, Haner wrote: "Ina baked bread and pies and cake today. Allie went with Charley Shepardson to the schoolhouse up west to see a Christmas tree - but it was all over with when they got there."

Timing was critical during an era when Christmas trees were lighted with small candles clipped onto the branches. The event might last but 15 or 20 minutes. A few wealthy families may have erected Christmas trees in their homes, but from the 1860s to the end of the century the usual means of viewing a Christmas tree was in a communal setting - at a schoolhouse, church or grange hall, where participants placed their gifts on the tree for public viewing. George Reynolds of Berrien Springs deviated from his usual Christmas wood chopping by 1863 to record in his diary entries the growing acceptance of the Christmas tree concept in that community, the Berrien County seat until 1894:

> *1863 December 24 A tolerable fine day. Was a Christmas tree over to the court house - distributed the presents in the evening.*

1874 December 24 Christmas tree at the Lutheran Church, Prayer Meeting at ours (United Brethren).

1875 December 24 Christmas tree at church and Grange Hall.

December 25 Got me a cloak on the Christmas tree last night.

1876 December 25 Had a very large turnout to our Christmas tree. Went off very pleasant. Lutherans had a Christmas house, ours was a Christmas arch.

1877 December 24 Christmas tree at the U.B. Church this evening. Willie went down. One out west at the Grange Hall and one over the river.

December 25 Christmas tree in our church. Quite a full house. My (Sunday) school class presented me with a very nice motto "I know that my redeemer lives."

Once Christmas had been widely accepted the gift giving generally remained modest by modern standards with presents being often hand made and utilitarian in nature. The diary entries of George C. Adams, a farmer from Kalamazoo County's Comstock Township, indicate that he resisted the Christmas spirit for nine years beginning in 1867. In 1876, he gave in, procrastinating, however, until Christmas day to do his holiday shopping. He itemized his expenditures:

2 quarts oysters 70 cents
hooks for pictures 5 cents
cord for picture frames 25 cents
plans for motto frames 20 cents
thimble for wife 50 cents
Total Christmas expenses $1.70

This ca. 1910 Santa eschewed reindeer for a new-fangled "aeroplane."

Fourteen-year-old Frank Stuart of Schoolcraft Township, Kalamazoo County, recorded the gifts his family received on Christmas morning 1879: "I got a lantern - Arthur a diary - Chas a knife - Father a pocket book - Mother a scarf - Libbie a book - Lena a doll and a set of silver."

Yet even with such modest gift giving, by the 1870s and 1880s Christmas had begun to take on a hint of the importance for retailers it would gradually achieve over the next century. Washington Engle who had listened to a lecture on dyspepsia during Christmas Eve, 1856, had settled in Hartford where he operated a general store to supplement his medical practice. On December 24, 1881, he recorded: "I am at store very busy selling goods for Christmas - 74 dollars taken in."

The Twentieth Century brought a continuing evolution in Michiganders' celebration of Christmas. Despite the heavy financial outlay and the pressure of trying to do too much in too little time, few would trade our gala modern tradition for the austere days of Christmas past. But in case anyone contemplates doing that, consider George DeLano's terse diary entry for Monday, December 25, 1882, "At home all day - the girls are washing."■

VIII

THE HUSSEYS OF BATTLE CREEK

There are times, when moiling among the detritus of the past, that an historian feels a faint tug of his sleeve as a quavering voice from the grave whispers - "do me." It happened in 1995, when rummaging through an antique shop in Marshall I was drawn to a volume bound in brown cloth labeled *Autobiography of Benjamin Hallowell*. A Quaker minister, Hallowell, I soon learned, had been a college president in Virginia. Robert E. Lee had studied under him. But what actually convinced me to purchase the book was the inscription written in a shaky hand on the flyleaf - "Willie Merritt. From my beloved Husband's Library - He always felt a great interest in thee dear boy, and I want thou should have something that was his, and have selected this autobiography of a good man, whom he loved and respected. In love. Sarah E. Hussey. Battle Creek. Jan. 24th 1889."

The Merritt name I remembered as that of a prominent Battle Creek family of Quaker pioneer farmers and entrepreneurs. William Guest Merritt, the grandson of one of Battle Creek's founders who had emigrated there from New York State in 1835, was 18-years-old in 1889. Sarah Hussey, I immediately recognized as the wife of Erastus Hussey, the famous Quaker conductor of Battle Creek's station on the Underground Railroad. Intent on

Sarah Hussey in 1877.

other projects, I ignored that faint tug of my sleeve and shelved the volume. But sometimes when I passed that shelf, I swear I heard a faint rustling of silken skirts and a ghostly whisper, "write about me."

Fast forward a dozen years when Vaughn Baber, a long-time friend and proprietor of an antiquarian bookshop in Kalamazoo, offered me a small pile of mostly beat up old volumes he had bought from a family moving out of town. These were the residue of what he was unable to sell on E-Bay. He named a fair price, and I brought the lot after a cursory examination.

That evening I pored over my new acquisitions more closely. A leather bound autograph book from the 1870s proved of particular interest. Over the years I had looked through dozens of these souvenir pieces hoping to find something of Michigan history interest, with no real success. This one had belonged to Eddie Wildman, who evidently traveled a good deal as there were inscriptions signed by friends and family in Massachusetts, Maine, Rhode Island, Illinois, Wisconsin, Iowa, Colorado, and South Dakota from the early 1870s to the 1890s.

Then I found it - three pages devoted to a 24-line poem about America's role in the world and reading in part:

> *The Best! yea Best, save one foul blot,*
> *One stain upon her history's pages.*
> *One dark disgrace! O tell it not,*
> *To blight her name in future ages.....*
> *That o'er our "Free" and "Happy" land,*
> *Oppression wields her iron sway*
> *And waves her dark and loathsome wand*
> *To cloud our country's brightest day.*

The antislavery verses were signed "Sarah E. Hussey. Battle Creek. April 1st 1878." A notation in her hand testified that the poem had originally been written for the *Liberty Press*, an Abolitionist periodical published by her husband in Battle Creek until some slavery sympathizer set fire to the printing office and burned it to the ground in 1849.

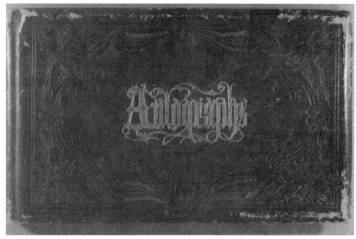

The Autograph Album.

The only other inscription signed by someone from Michigan occurs near the back of the book and is written upside-down on the page. There, on June 5, 1877, Erastus Hussey, himself, had scrawled out some of the philosophy that had guided him through his long life of fighting oppression:

> *Follow closely the teachings of the Divine light that God has implanted in thy soul as a guide to all thy actions and thy happiness will be ensured. Plant thy standard of Reform on the highest plain of Truth, Justice and Human Rights and God will enable thee to overcome all opposition. Always do right according to the truth made manifest in thy understanding and leave the consequences to the power that controls all things.*
>
> *Rather stand up assured with conscious pride alone, than err with millions on thy side.*

The slight tug from the past had become an irresistible pull. Born in Cayuga County, New York, on December 5, 1800, Hussey spent his childhood on a farm on the east shore of the big "finger lake" named Cayuga. He received little in the way of formal education, but read as many books as he could lay his hands on. As a teenager, he taught school in the winter and farmed the rest of the year. Having saved up $250, in 1824, like many another western New Yorker of his generation, he set off for Michigania. Walking to Buffalo, Hussey boarded the *Independence*, than the only steamship on Lake Erie, and landed in Detroit on September 25, 1824. After exploring the territory for two weeks, he returned to Detroit and bought 160 acres in what would become Plymouth Township, Wayne County.

In 1827, Hussey returned to Cayuga County to marry 19-year-old Sarah Eddy Bowen. He brought her to the primitive log cabin on their homestead. They survived

Erastus Hussey in 1877.

a bout of the "ague," as Michigan pioneers called mosquito-borne malaria, built a better log dwelling and in January, 1828, Sarah gave birth to their only child, Susan.

In 1836, Hussey sold the Wayne County farm at a handsome profit and, following a tour of the east, he cast his lot with Battle Creek in 1838. He first manufactured shoes and boots, but a year later opened up a dry goods store. Active in the political arena, Hussey promoted numerous reforms. He became one of the first to campaign for a high school in Battle Creek supported by a general tax. He served as town clerk for three terms, and, in 1849, he became one of only five candidates running under the banner of the short-lived Liberty Party to win election to the Michigan House of Representatives. In 1854, Hussey helped found the Republican Party in Jackson, and that fall he was elected to the state senate. The following year he introduced the "personal liberty bill" which narrowly passed the state house and senate and outlawed the seizure of fugitive slaves in Michigan.

In the 1820s, Levi Coffin, a Quaker from Cincinnati, had become involved in a highly secret system for assisting runaway slaves to reach freedom in Canada.

Largely manned by Quakers, courageous stalwarts of the Abolitionist Movement, it became known as the Underground Railroad. In 1840, Coffin and others sought to better organize the route through Michigan which led to Detroit, the primary entrance to Canada. Across the Detroit River, east of Windsor, in fact, a number of runaway slave colonies had sprung up.

John Cross, from Indiana, asked Hussey, then one of only six antislavery advocates in Battle Creek, to become station master there. He readily agreed, and a month later the first runaways appeared at his store and living quarters on Main Street. Hussey, described how the Underground Railroad functioned during an interview in 1885:

> *Our work was conducted with the greatest secrecy. After crossing the Ohio River the fugitives separated, but came together on the main line and were conducted through Indiana and Michigan. Stations were established every fifteen or sixteen miles. The slaves were secreted in the woods, barns and cellars during the daytime and carried through in the night. All traveling was done in the dark. The station keepers received no pay... It was all out of sympathy for the escaped slaves and from principle. We were working for humanity.*

Two branches of the Underground Railroad traversed Michigan. The shortest ran from Adrian to Detroit, but the most heavily traveled route began in the Quaker settlement near Cassopolis then stretched across the state with stations in Schoolcraft, Climax, Battle Creek, Marshall, Albion, Parma, Jackson, Michigan Center, Leoni, Grass Lake, Francisco, Dexter, Scio, Ann Arbor, Geddes (a Washtenaw County ghost town), Ypsilanti, Plymouth, Swartzburg and Detroit.

The Husseys were awakened many a night by a rap

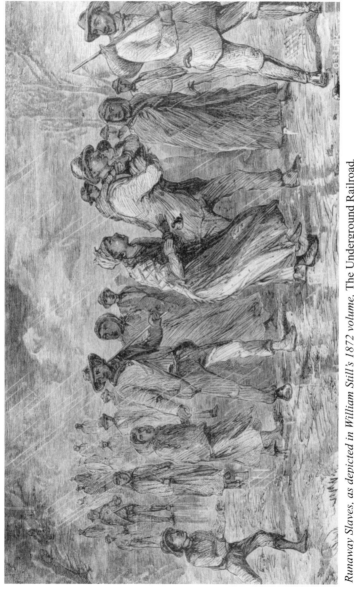

Runaway Slaves, as depicted in William Still's 1872 volume, The Underground Railroad.

on the door and the whispered passwords: "Can you give shelter and protection to one or more persons?" Erastus, Sarah and daughter Susan then hustled a band of frightened fugitives inside, provided food and drink, mended their torn garments and hid them, until, under cover of darkness the following night, Hussey drove the runaways in his wagon to the station in Marshall.

They usually arrived in small groups of less than four, but the Husseys never forgot the excitement during a night in 1847 when 45 fugitives arrived at once. A raid by Kentucky slave owners upon the Quaker settlement in Cass County had caused all resident runaway slaves to flee at once. In the middle of the night a messenger had arrived to inform Hussey that the fugitives would arrive two hours later. "What to do I did not know," Hussey recalled, and Sarah was sick in bed. He quickly conferred with three other Battle Creek Abolitionists and they secured the use of an unoccupied dwelling, rustled up a sack of flour, potatoes and pork and were ready when:

> *We heard them coming over the West Main Street Bridge. Everybody had heard of their coming and every man, woman and child in the city was upon the street and it looked as if a circus was coming to town. It was a lovely moonlight night. There were nine white men with them who acted as guards. Ahead of them rode Zachariah Shugart, the old Quaker, with his broad-brimmed white hat and mounted on a fine horse. He met me in front of my house and shook hands with me. I told him of my arrangements. He took off his white hat and with a military air and voice said: "Right about face!" They all about-faced and marched down to the house and took possession. The next morning the majority of them went on to Canada, but a few remained, who became honored citizens and well-known.*

Despite attempts at secrecy, it eventually became common knowledge in the slave states that Battle Creek was a major station on the Underground Railroad. Hussey "expected every day to be arrested." Once he received word that 30 armed men were on their way to capture the slaves in Battle Creek. Hussey had 500 broadsides printed up, stating that "we were prepared to meet them, and advised them to stay away." At Niles the southerners read one of the bills and turned back.

From 1840 to about 1855, the Hussey family gave refuge to and guided to safety more than 1,000 runaway slaves.

Erastus Hussey died at the age of 88, and three days later his widow presented young Willie Merritt with the keepsake volume. Ten years later, Sarah joined her husband in Battle Creek's Oak Hill Cemetery. Merritt

The Hussey's first Battle Creek homestead, a genuine Underground Railroad station.

died in 1950 at the age of 80, and his grave lies not far from the Husseys.

The sketch of the Husseys's lives in the 1904 *Biographical Review of Calhoun County* concludes with a fitting tribute: "The world is the better for their having lived. Who can measure their influence or gauge the good which they wrought! Their memory remains as a blessed benediction to those who knew them and to all who live after them will the fruits of their labor be apparent."

And more than a century later, Erastus and Sarah continue to speak through a flyleaf inscription and the pages of an old autograph album.■

IX

THE DRUMMER BOY OF CHICKAMAUGA

Brandishing his cavalry sword, the Confederate colonel galloped up to the tiny twelve-year old soldier and yelled, "Stop, you little Yankee devil!" Or maybe he said, "Surrender, you damned little Yankee!" Still another source published during the height of Victorian morality has the colonel crying "Surrender you little_____!"

What happened next all three sources agree on. Johnny Clem of the 22nd Michigan Infantry Regiment leveled the diminutive musket he had been furnished and shot the colonel off his mount. Dripping with journalistic circumlocution typical of the era, a contemporary newspaper account put it "the proud colonel tumbled dead from his horse, his lips stained with the syllables of vile reproach he had flung upon a mother's grave in the hearing of her child," thus also giving a pretty good hint of what the Confederate's expletive-deleted had been.

Variant epithets comprise but one of the difficulties in determining the real story of what happened to "the most famous drummer-boy of the Civil War" during the bloody Battle of Chickamauga, Georgia, on September 20, 1863.

Born August 13, 1851, in Newark, Ohio, John Clem ran away from home in May, 1861, a month after the bombardment of Fort Sumter and President Lincoln's call for 75,000 volunteers to suppress "the insurrection." When 9-year-old Clem offered his services as a drummer boy to a company commander of the 3rd

Johnny Clem, " The Drummer Boy of Chickamauga."

Ohio Volunteer Infantry, the officer laughed in his face and sneered, "I'm not enlisting infants." Actually, throughout the war fully 10,000 soldiers 17 or younger enlisted in the Union Army - at least 25 were less than 11-years old.

Undeterred by the Ohio officer's rude rebuke, the patriotic tyke tried the 22nd Michigan Infantry which had been recruited in the counties of Oakland, Livingston, Macomb, St. Clair, Lapeer and Sanilac and organized in Pontiac. During the late summer of 1862, under command of Col. Moses Wisner, former governor of the state, the regiment traveled through Ohio to the Kentucky front lines. Again an officer rebuffed the lad. Still determined to be a soldier, Clem tagged along with the regiment, making himself useful in camp, and during the march he "acted just the same as a drummer-boy." He finally wore down the officers' resistance and while he was too young to be formally sworn in they donated a regular private's pay of $13 a month out of their own funds to the little drummer.

Clem soon became adept at playing the big snare drum swung against his left hip on the march. He learned to rat-a-tat-tat reveille, mess call, double quick and tattoo. He also increasingly played solemn music at the burials of men of the 22nd Michigan killed in battle or the many more who died of disease or wounds in the hospital. On occasion he drummed out of camp a disgraced soldier, head shaved and shorn of his buttons, who had been convicted of some offense such as stealing from comrades. When not drumming, Clem gathered firewood, helped the cook on "K.P.," carried messages from officer to officer and performed other light duties. Not so light a duty was that of assisting surgeons as they sawed off wounded soldiers' limbs.

Another of Clem's activities, at which he proved adept, was to help forage off the land to supplement the regiment's rations. Because the government sought to preserve civilian support, Col. Charles Doolittle, commander of the brigade in Kentucky, issued an order against killing stray hogs. Shortly after, Doolittle heard a musket go off not far from camp. He investigated and found Clem red handed with a hog he had shot. "John," said the colonel as recorded in the 1880 publication *Michigan in the War:* "Don't you know it is against orders to kill hogs?" "I know it," replied

A contemporary print poignantly portrays a mother kissing her little drummer boy goodbye.

the fast thinking youth, "but I don't intend to let any rebel hogs bite me!"

During the Battle of Shiloh, Clem won national attention as "Johnny Shiloh." When an artillery round shattered his drum he continued to bravely face the enemy. To save his troops from defeat, General Ulysses Grant rode up and shouted, "Don't let a boy and his General stand there and fight alone" - or so the widely circulated story ran. "The Drummer Boy of Shiloh," based on the event, became one of the war's most popular songs. The incident also inspired a Vaudeville play which continued to jerk the tears from audiences well into the twentieth century. Later came James A. Rhodes' book *Johnny Shiloh: A Novel of the Civil War* and a popular Walt Disney movie of the 1960s.

Alas, here is where historical accuracy ruins a good story. The Battle of Shiloh, Tennessee, was fought on April 6 and 7, 1862, about four months before the 22nd Michigan Infantry was even mustered into service. Whoever that brave drummer boy was, if indeed the incident actually occurred, he was not John Clem. It seems that a newspaper article published about Johnny Shiloh in 1871 and erroneously naming Clem as the hero somehow found its way into his service records. Successive ranks of historians accepted the story without verification until the appearance of Dennis M. Keesee's finely researched tome about youthful Union soldiers in 2003.

If Clem was not Johnny Shiloh, was he really the "Drummer-Boy of Chickamauga?" The answer is yes and no. Clem and the 22nd Michigan Infantry definitely fought bravely at the Battle of Chickamauga which pitted Maj. Gen. William S. Rosecrans's Army of the Cumberland against Gen. Braxton Bragg's Confederate troops. Major General George H. Thomas's stubborn stand around Snodgrass Hill saved the battle from becoming a Federal rout. Thomas became known as "The Rock of Chickamauga," and a popular poem of that title written by Dr. William B. Hamilton, a lieutenant in the unit, named the men of the 22nd Michigan Infantry:

> *Let rebels boast their Stonewall brave*
> *Who fell to fill a traitor's grave,*

We have a hero grander far,
The Union was his guiding star,
The 'Rock of Chickamauga.'

Sons of Macomb and broad St. Clair,
And Oakland's rolling fields were there.
And now they tell, with patriot pride,
How that great day they fought beside
The 'Rock of Chickamauga'.

Of the 455 men of the 22nd Michigan Infantry engaged in the battle, only 66 survived unscathed. Scores of those captured would later die in the horrible Confederate prison at Andersonville, Georgia. During the battle, Clem served as a regimental marker, hoisting the guidon that allowed the company to form in alignment. It was a particularly dangerous position because enemy sharpshooters frequently targeted regimental battle flag holders.

The story of his shooting the Confederate colonel, however, was fabricated by journalists. Clem was wounded slightly by Confederate shrapnel and captured. When being marched behind the line, he fell out and feigned being dead until the enemy left the field. He eventually made his way back to the remnants of his regiment, walking ten miles throughout the night.

Lionized by the national press as the "Drummer Boy of Chickamauga," Clem's story gained unwarranted details with each subsequent telling. Although he never actually claimed to have done more than what really transpired, he became a celebrity, posing for studio portraits in his colorfully tailored uniform and miniature rifle. Some sources claim the popular song, "When Johnny Comes Marching Home Again," was based on his exploits, real or imagined. At the height of his popularity Clem added the middle name Lincoln. He won promotion to lance sergeant in May 1863 and, until his discharge in September of 1864, continued to serve with the 22nd Michigan Infantry as a courier.

Unlike that of many another Civil War hero, Clem's story did not end with the Confederate surrender at Appomattox

Battles and Leaders of the Civil (1884) contains an engraving of the Confederate line in the Chickamauga Woods.

Courthouse on April 12, 1865. Gen. Thomas took the boy under his wing and helped finance his attendance at the Newark, Ohio, High School where he graduated in 1870. Clem entered the regular army as a second lieutenant in the 24th Infantry the following year. He steadily rose up the ranks, winning promotion to captain in 1882, major in 1895 and lieutenant colonel in 1901.

In 1916, Clem retired as a two star general, the last Civil War veteran to leave active service. He died at his San Antonio, Texas, home in 1937. His gravestone at Arlington National Cemetery documents in marble that he was indeed "The Drummer Boy of Chickamauga." ■

John L. Clem, aged 11 years.

X

CHAPLAIN CORBY OF THE IRISH BRIGADE

Before the tall Celtic cross with a recumbent greyhound carved into its marble base, stood grizzled Father William Corby, former chaplain of the famed Irish Brigade. It was July 2, 1888, and the surviving member of the brigade, some with empty sleeves, eye patches and crutches, had gathered at Gettysburg to celebrate the 25th anniversary of their role in the bloody three-day battle which claimed 50,000 casualties and ultimately decided the outcome of the Civil War.

Recalling many a brave exploit, Corby addressed his fellow veterans at the dedication of their regimental monument. As he gazed over their gray-headed ranks he was moved to say, "Here is what is left of us; where are the others?" And with that query, the answer to which he knew too well, the priest choked up, unable to speak for several minutes. Many of the tough old veterans unashamedly let the tears roll down their cheeks, as well.

As Corby struggled to regain composure, a flood of memories welled up. He heard again the dreadful boom of artillery and the crackle of a thousand muskets. He saw a captain from Michigan, a friend he had been talking to seconds before, torn in two by a cannon ball. He shuddered at the thought of towering piles of limbs before the surgeon's tent after the battle. He remembered his brief interview with a sad-eyed President

Lincoln as he pleaded for mercy for a soldier in his unit sentenced to die, the clemency that was not granted and the face of that soldier as he heard his confession before the execution.

Corby had been born in Detroit on October 2, 1833, the fifth child of a traditionally large Irish Catholic family. His father, Daniel Corby, had emigrated from Kings County, Ireland, to Canada as a young man. In 1824 he married Elizabeth Stapleton in Montreal. Two years later the Corbys settled in

Father Corby ca. 1880.

Detroit, the capital of Michigan Territory, then a sparsely settled Ultima Thule branded nothing but an interminable swamp. Over the succeeding forty years the elder Corby carved out a lucrative career as a civil engineer and real estate dealer, ultimately becoming one of Wayne County's wealthiest proprietors. A devout Catholic who combined piety with shrewdness in business, Corby helped found numerous English speaking parishes in the Detroit environs.

His son William received a primary education in Detroit public schools and, following in his father's footsteps, joined the real estate concern at the age of sixteen. The younger Corby also grew to love the Catholic Church and aspired to the priesthood. In 1853, Corby sent William and three of his brothers to the fledgling college of Notre Dame, Indiana, founded ten years before by Congregation of Holy Cross priest Father Edward Sorin.

Sorin took a liking to the young Irish student, abetted perhaps by William's gift to the college in 1855 of a plot of land in Detroit which sold for $5,000 a few years later. Corby entered the novitiate in 1857 and three years later took his final vows as priest. The newly ordained Corby celebrated his first mass before his proud father and family in the old parish church in Detroit.

In the meantime, under Sorin's guidance Corby rose within the hierarchy at Notre Dame. In 1859, he become prefect of discipline, cracking the whip to maintain the regimented life style at the college. By 1861, he also served as director of Notre Dame's Manual Labor School and pastor of South Bend's incipient St. Patrick's parish.

When the Civil War broke out that year, Sorin dared not officially commit the college to the Union cause, in part because of numerous Southerners in the student body, but clearly his sympathies lay with the North. During the war he sent seven Notre Dame priests to serve as chaplains in Union units and more than 80 Sisters of the Holy Cross as nurses in Federal hospitals. In the summer of 1861, Sorin ordered Father James Dillon to Washington, D.C., where he became chaplain to the nearly 3,000 Irish-Catholic soldiers, largely from New York City, who had rushed to enlist in the Irish Brigade commanded by colorful Col. Thomas Francis Meagher. In an era when the Irish huddled in the nation's socio-economic basement and Catholics were perceived by nativists as a threat to the Republic, such red-blooded patriotism, as well as the Irish Brigade's subsequent record of valor throughout the war, would help propel the recent immigrants up the American ethnic elevator.

Officers of the Irish Brigade posed while on the Virginia Peninsula in 1862. Father Corby is seated on the right (courtesy United States Army Military History Institute).

In the fall of 1861 Dillon requested additional help, and Corby joined him in Camp California near Alexandria, Virginia. The brigade remained in garrison that first winter, the men itching to inflict on those "Johnny Rebs" some of their time-honored Hibernian pugnacity. Corby recalled: "During that winter we spent our time in much the same way as parish priests do, except in this - we had no old women to bother us, or pew rent to collect." Finally, on March 5, 1862, the brigade received orders to march to the front, in the direction of the wreckage of the Battle of Bull Run. Disappointed to discover that the enemy had vacated the vicinity, the brigade boarded transports and landed on the Virginia Peninsula, unfortunately in the malaria-ridden Chicahominy Swamps, where disease killed more than bullets. While ministering to the sick, Corby contracted malaria and was himself hospitalized for two weeks.

On June 1, 1862, the Irish Brigade received its baptism by fire at the Battle of Fair Oaks. Contemporary historian John T. Headley described what happened when the Confederate infantrymen attacked: "The Irish Brigade advanced with their well-known war shout, and closed with fearful ferocity on the foe, and for an hour mowed them down almost by companies." As the war progressed, more than one Confederate officer would record, "the Irish fight like devils" and "here comes that damned green flag again" in reference to the regimental battle flag, Kelly green and emblazoned with a golden harp. Nevertheless, heroic charges took a fearful toll on the Irish as well. At the subsequent Seven Days Campaign in Virginia, when McClellan's and Lee's armies slugged it out, the Irish Brigade, according to Corby, "left 700 of its bravest officers and men on the bloody fields behind."

On September 17, 1862, at the Battle of Antietam, Maryland, "the bloodiest single day in the Civil War," the Irish Brigade led the initial Union infantry charge. Corby recalled his role:

> *I gave rein to my horse, and let him go at full gallop till I reached the front of the brigade, and, passing along the line, told the men to make an Act of Contrition. As they were coming toward me,*

"double quick," I had time only to wheel my horse for an instant toward them and gave my poor men a hasty absolution, and rode with Gen. Meagher into the battle. In twenty or thirty minutes after this absolution, 506 of these very men lay on the field, either dead or seriously wounded... I shall never forget how wicked the whiz of the enemy's bullets seemed as we advanced into that battle. A soon as my men began to fall, I dismounted and began to hear their confessions on the spot - every instant bullets whipping past my head.

March of 1863 found the Irish Brigade in camp near Falmouth, Va., during a lull in the fighting. The carnage it had suffered would not prevent the brigade from staging a rollicking Saint Patrick's Day celebration, considered by a number of participants as "the most significant non-combat event that the

Chaplains Corby and Ouellet were nearly killed by Confederate cannon shots before Petersburg in 1864.

An 1863 artist's conception of the steeplechase at the Irish Brigade's gala St. Patrick's Day celebration.

Army of the Potomac ever experienced." Some 10,000 troops as well as high ranking officers, including Maj. Gen. Joseph Hooker, in command, attended the festivities.

Corby launched the ceremonies by celebrating mass in a rustic pine-bough chapel fashioned for the occasion. The event featured army bands blaring liturgical music, parading contingents of Irish soldiers in spit-shine finery and "a consecration announced by cannon fire rather than bells."

A "Grand Irish Brigade Steeple Chase" followed, providing "squireens from the old sod" a chance to display their riding skills. A number of soldiers had crowded beneath the grand stand erected for the dignitaries. Gen. Meagher galloped up and shouted in his brogue: "Stand from under! If that stage gives way, you will be crushed by four tons of major-generals."

During the ensuing feast, the officers downed "35 hams, a side of ox roasted, an entire pig stuffed with boiled turkeys and an unlimited number of chickens, ducks and small game" washed down with eight baskets of champagne, ten gallons of rum and 22 of whiskey. The enlisted men enjoyed a special ration of a half pint of fiery liquor and, they being Irish and it being St. Patrick's Day, it was noted that "many men somehow got hold of more than their allotted share."

On May 2, 1863, the Irish Brigade was back in the heat of battle at Chancellorsville, Va. Corby was conducting Sunday morning mass when the call to advance came. He had only time to shout as his sermon, "God bless and protect my men." The bloody four-day battle claimed 30,000 Union and Confederate causalities, including, of irreparable loss to the South, the "friendly fire" death of Gen. Stonewall Jackson.

It was at Gettysburg, however, that Corby immortalized his role as chaplain of the Irish Brigade. On July 2, 1863, the second day of the battle, the brigade had marched 13 miles to take a position atop Cemetery Ridge. Opposite, about a mile away, stood the Rebel force on Seminary Ridge. The Union defenders were being pushed back by Confederate charges when the order came for the brigade to advance down the hill for a rendezvous with death in the Rose Wheatfield below.

Paul Henry Wood's 1890 painting, "Absolution Under Fire," depicted Father Corby at Gettysburg (courtesy Snite Museum of Art, University of Notre Dame).

Corby quickly leaped atop a boulder and addressed the brigade. He explained that each was about to receive the benefit of the absolution and urged them to do their duty toward "the high and sacred nature of their trust as soldiers and the noble object for which they fought." Then, every man before him, Catholic and non-Catholics alike, fell on his knees with his head bowed.

Stretching his right hand toward the brigade, Corby recited the Latin words of the absolution: *"Dominus nostu Jesus Christus vos absolvant... in nomini Patris, et Felii, et Spiritus Sancti, Amen."* Thirty years later Corby recalled: "I do not think there was a man in the brigade, who did not offer up a heart-felt prayer. For some, it was their last: they knelt there in their grave clothes." The Irish Brigade lost fully half of the men in some individual regiments at Gettysburg.

For nearly three years, Corby ministered to men of the Irish Brigade as they served in the major campaigns of the war, until in September, 1864, Sorin called him back to Notre Dame. That urgent business finished, Corby rejoined his men in the trenches around Petersburg in the closing days of the war.

Returning to Notre Dame, he became vice president of the college in 1865. The following year he assumed the presidency. In 1872 he left to establish a branch institution at Watertown, Wisconsin. From 1877 to 1881 Corby served a second stint as president of Notre Dame. When most of the college structures burned to the ground in 1879, he inspired the rebuilding efforts, earning him the title "Second Founder of Notre Dame."

Efforts to convince Congress to award the "Fighting Chaplain" the Medal of Honor in the 1880s came to naught. In 1893, Corby published his account of the war, *Memoirs of Chaplain Life*. Five years later he died of pneumonia at Notre Dame. Stoop-shouldered veterans from the local Grand Army of the Republic post bore his coffin, shrouded in the green flag of the Irish Brigade, to the cemetery on the shore of St. Mary's Lake.

Gen. St. Clair Mulholland, one of the soldiers who had knelt before Corby at Gettysburg, led a campaign to erect a statue

The statue of Father Corby erected at Gettysburg in 1910.

in the chaplain's honor at Gettysburg. In 1910, veterans gathered again for the dedication of a bronze likeness of Corby, arm upraised in delivering the absolution, the sole sacerdotal monument in the battlefield. A year later, an identical statue was unveiled in front of Corby Hall on the Notre Dame campus. That figure with raised arm has inspired irreverent Notre Dame students, more versed in the "Fighting Irish's" gridiron exploits than martial heritage, to dub the statue, "Fair Catch Corby." ∎

XI

BOOK HAWKERS & DOOR KNOCKERS

If Annie Nelles had been in a worse predicament during her short but miserable life she could not remember when. True, heretofore her lot "had been one constant scene of clouds and darkness, with only here and there a ray of sunshine, which served but to make darkness, both preceding and following it, more dense, impenetrable and frightful." But now, penniless in Detroit in 1866 and masquerading as a young widow, of which the recent Civil War had produced so many, she labored long hours as a housekeeper at wages of a paltry $2 a week.

The constant brooding over her fate had brought on a bout of depression which deepened into physical illness. She took to her bed from which "it was thought for some time she would never rise." During the sickness she raved feverishly about her previous life, the details of which she had shamefully hidden from her kindly employers. She babbled of her birth in 1837, daughter of a wealthy planter near Atlanta, Georgia. Alas, that brief, happy childhood would soon fade. Her father died in 1843, and by the time she was 13 her mother and three siblings lay in graves beside his.

The benevolent uncle and aunt who took her in died soon after. The shock of that unrelenting mortality

Annie Nelles, who climbed the ladder of success by hawking books door to door.

resulted in "brain fever," and for 11 weeks she languished in a coma. Had not her brother periodically held a mirror to her nostrils to prove she still breathed, she would have been buried alive.

On her 17th birthday she married Eugene Giles, a handsome young widower introduced to her by the man appointed her guardian. After their first child died in infancy, Giles took to the bottle and during drunken jags gambled away all their possessions. As if that were not enough, shortly thereafter came a knock on the door to reveal Giles' first wife whom he had deserted some eight years before.

Annie fled the bigamist, settling in Detroit where she ran a boarding house. Two years later she spotted Giles walking the streets of Detroit, and she quickly packed up and boarded the first train for Chicago. There she managed another boarding house. Some time later she was wooed by one of her boarders, a seemingly fine young man. She married Frank Ford in 1866 and enjoyed a brief period of matrimonial bliss. That is, until she found a series of love letters tucked in a jacket Ford had left on a chair, shadowed him and witnessed his assignation with a "woman of the night." Annie gulped a vial of laudanum, and only the skill of a pair of physicians working on her all night saved the distraught woman from a successful suicide.

When her health had been restored, her husband, now unmasked as the brute he was, connived a complete separation through cruel treatment. Annie left Chicago with a trunk and a measly $15 Ford doled out to her. She tarried briefly in Niles where she worked as a housekeeper. But she found the haughty contempt of her employer intolerable. Returning to Detroit, she secured another housekeeping position, this time with a decent and considerate family. After Annie had recovered from her latest sickness, during which she had deliriously blurted out her many misfortunes, the sympathetic family consoled her on how she might recoup her life.

Obviously, working as a maid at $2 a week was not the answer. And it was an era when most of the other occupations thought suitable for women; seamstress, laundress, cook, teacher, etc. offered little better financial rewards. But there was one opportunity, if a woman possessed sufficient talent, that might prove otherwise. It was the father of the household who suggested to Annie - that she became a "book agent."

In her popular guide to choosing a career for women Mr. M. L. Rayne of Detroit thought no profession more suitable than that of a "lady book canvasser."

The period after the Civil War through the Gay Nineties emerged as the golden age of door-to-door book selling, thanks in part to a ready supply of ex-soldiers, many without limbs, hungry to make a living as best they could. In addition to salesmen proudly sporting Grand Army of the Republic badges, aging clergymen, spinsters and widows, schoolteachers in the summertime and college students swelled the ranks of the thousands knocking on doors while armed with thin prospectuses containing samples of the illustrations, text and other features of the thick volumes yet to be published. These itinerant sales people cajoled householders into signing on the dotted line of the blank pages, conveniently provided at the rear of each prospectus, after choosing the binding they preferred; garishly gilded cloth, half leather or full Morocco, ranging from $2.50 - $10 or more, 25 to 30 times the value in modern terms. If sales were sufficient to warrant publishing the work, weeks later the "canvasser" would deliver the books and collect payment.

Gen. Ulysses S. Grant's *Memoirs* published in two volumes by Mark Twain's Charles L. Webster Company in 1885 and sold exclusively by wandering agents achieved a press run of 350,000 sets. On the other hand, Warner, Beers & Co.'s *Atlas of Berrien County* projected in 1885 and James L. Smith's *History of Michigan* slated to appear in Muskegon in 1909 exist only as prospectuses. Not enough patrons signed up to make publication a reality.

By the early 1870s the New York *Tribune* declared "there is not a cross-road in any part of the country that is not at some time visited by the book agent." Publishers in Chicago, Detroit, St. Louis and other eastern and midwestern cities broadcast agents by the hundreds into the hinterlands. But the many firms in Hartford, Conn., rendered that city the center of the subscription publishing industry. The J.B. Burr and Hyde Company, headquartered at 114 Asylum St. in Hartford, published a long list of titles popular in the 1870s including: Officer

Geo S. McWatters' *Knots Untied*; or *Ways and By-Ways in the Hidden Life of American Detectives*; P.T. Barnum's *Struggles and Triumphs*; Mathew Hale Smith's *Twenty Years Among the Bulls and Bears of Wall Street* and Mrs. Stephen M. Griswold's *A Woman's Pilgrimage to the Holy Land*. Burr and Hyde proudly described how it conducted business:

> *The method we adopt of selling books exclusively by canvassing agent is an established, legitimate and reputable branch of the book trade, and is the medium through which the most popular books have been and are circulated. Through its agency, many of the most reliable, instructive and entertaining books published for the past ten years or more, have reached the public, and it is generally conceded that it will ultimately supersede the book stores as a means of giving circulation to first class books of a standard character.*

If Burr and Hyde seemed somewhat defensive in their testimonial there was good reason. The thousands of agents that inundated the countryside had begun to take on the character of nuisances. Charles B. Lewis, a humorous Detroit *Free Press* writer of the 1870s, recounted his experiences fending off swarms of book agents:

> *He or she will call on you to sell you this book. He may be a pale-faced young man, standing on the verge of the grave, as it were, or she may be an interesting young lady with freckles on her nose and a forlorn look.*
>
> *Do not be deceived. They will have a deceptive story at their tongue's end, and as*

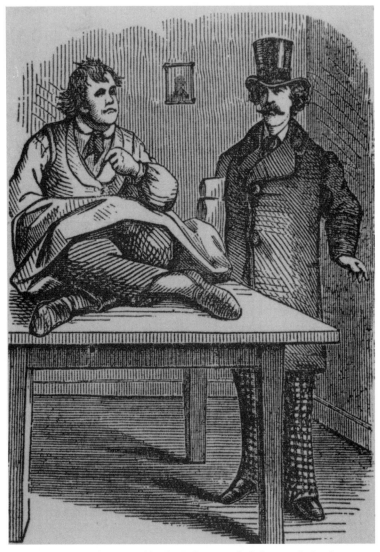

Detroit newspaper humorist Charles B. Lewis included a cut of a book agent attempting to sell to a tailor.

> they corner you they will get off something like this:
>
> "Let me put your name down for this book - best book published for years - selling like hot cakes - first edition exhausted in 24 minutes - author known all over the country - orders being received from China, Japan, Madagascar and the Cape of Good Hope - sold only by subscription - write it right there on that line."
>
> Book agents will stick to their game like a burr to a boy's heel... Book agents have worn holes in my front door steps; they have unhinged my gate; they have aroused me from sleep, and have trailed me up and down and hung to me until I could offer no further objections.

The persistence of book salesmen moved the editor of the Grand Rapids *Daily Times* to dash off an angry column in 1874:

> The number of book agents is rapidly on the increase in the city and forms one colossal nuisance of the most unmitigated character. They are not content with pestering business men and annoying the people of "down town" but creep up into the resident districts, infest private houses, waylay honest citizens and almost torment the lives out of defenseless housekeepers. If the city authorities have no power to remove the mischief then let readers take the law into their own hands, buy an ugly dog, and "sic" him on first occasion.

Despite a growing reluctance to tolerate the hordes of book canvassers plying their trade, Mrs. M.L. Rayne,

Detroit authoress of the popular tome, *What Can A Woman Do*, published in her hometown in 1883, saw no reason why respectable women, single or married, should not take up the profession. She wrote:

> *It is doubtful if there is any work more especially suited to the taste and capacity of a bright, energetic woman, with a good fund of common sense about her, than the sale of subscription books throughout the country... There is nothing in the work to be ashamed*

Mrs. M. L. Rayne of Detroit.

> of... Some of these agents make as much as $2,000 a year.
>
> The true lady will compel every man into whose office or store she enters, to treat her as he would wish his own mother or sister to be treated at the hands of other men. She has a right to be heard; has just as good a right to demand a market for her goods as he has for his, and both parties must approach each other on the basis of mutual respect and tolerance.

It is a pleasant image - a dignified matron expostulating on the merits of a good book before a respectful businessman. And it may well have happened that way, sometimes. But for all the "wives and widows of lawyers, doctors, statesmen and army officers" whom Rayne assured her readers formed the bulk of lady book canvassers there survive numerous pathetic examples of women forced into the business because of heartfelt need. Witness an 1892 letter from Mrs. J. Honsberger of Charlotte to Laban D. Emery, who distributed alcohol and narcotics-laden elixirs from his hotel room on Kalamazoo's North Burdick Street:

> Enclosed please find $2.25 for 4 bottles of bitters and 2 cough medicines. I am not able to buy more at present for Mr. Honsberger has not been able to work for one year and I am obliged to canvas for a living. I have been working with books and since Christmas have been sick with La Grippe so if your medicine braces me up again I shall sell more.

Quack Emery disappeared from the *Kalamazoo City Directory* in 1896. Whatever happened to poor Mrs. Honsberger and her invalid husband remains an unanswered question.

An 1890s trade card depicts a successful book agent at work.

For Annie Nelles, we can record a more satisfying conclusion. The seed planted in her mind by that kindly employer - to attempt to sell books - spurred her to answer the following newspaper advertisement in 1866:

> *Wanted, agents, both ladies and gentlemen to canvass for "Tried and True, or Love and Loyalty," a new book destined to have an immense sale. Apply to W. J. Holland, 38 Lombard Block, Chicago.*

Early the next morning found Annie knocking at the Lombard Block office. She talked her way into being assigned the rights to sell the novel, a "romance of the Great Rebellion," in Peoria County, Illinois. Armed with a prospectus and wicker basket, she sold 40 copies at $2.75 each during her first week's work - a profit for her of $40. Naturally, her climb up the ladder of success varied from day to day. Sometimes scoring a sale was like pulling teeth, her own, as it turned out. A skinflint Peoria dentist, only ordered a copy of the novel for his wife after yanking a pair of the agent's teeth as payment.

But Annie was on her way, eventually securing exclusive sales rights for northern Indiana and the southern tier of Michigan counties. In addition to *Tried and True* she hawked the *Life of Lincoln*, E. A. Pollard's *The Lost Cause*, a history of the Civil War from a southern perspective, *The Children's Album*, *The Home Circle* and the *General History of Freemasonry in Europe*, a volume nearly irresistible to ambitious lawyers, politicians and businessmen in an era when membership in the Masonic order was sine qua non.

In 1867 Annie published an account of her own career, *The Life of a Book Agent*. Other novels and collections of short stories would follow. By 1892 her autobiography had gone through five editions.

The prospectus for Parson's Hand Book, *published in Battle Creek in 1882, included samples of the various bindings available, pebbled cloth at $4.00 and sheep leather at $5.00.*

The final chapter of Annie's story finds her comfortably ensconced in "a pleasant mansion in the midst of a beautiful grove, two and half miles from the city of Lexington, Kentucky," purchased with the proceeds of her success in banging on doors with subscription book in hand. ∎

Annie's competition included itinerant religious book sellers known as colporteurs.

XII

AGASSIZ REDUX & RED ROCK RICHES

It was a fortuitous meeting at Sault Ste. Marie on June 29, 1848, and one that would prove both symbolic and prophetic. Dr. Charles T. Jackson and his assistant, John Wells Foster, en route to conduct a survey of the Keweenaw copper country for the federal government, had arrived in the Sault that day. Louis Agassiz, who would depart on his scientific expedition to the north shore of Lake Superior the following morning, received valuable information about the geology of the south shore from the mineral surveyors. Agassiz's book, *Lake Superior*, the first scientific account of the big lake, would appear in 1850 and focus worldwide attention on the potential of its natural resources.

    The three volumes written by Jackson, Foster and another assistant, Josiah D. Whitney, were published by the federal government in 1849-1851, and they helped accelerate the Keweenaw copper rush that had been launched by the promotional efforts of State Geologist Douglass Houghton before the icy waters of Lake Superior claimed his life in 1845. Many fortunes would be made and lost in the copper country during the 1840s and 1850s. But the person who profited more then most from investment in the grandest mine of all, the Calumet and Hecla, would be none other than Agassiz's son Alexander. Nearly two decades and a terrible war which nearly destroyed the Union, and in which Michigan's mineral wealth played no small part, would pass before that.

Born in Neuchatel, Switzerland, in 1835, Agassiz, the son, was named after his mother's brother, Alexander Braun, an eminent German botanist. Another uncle, Maximillian Braun, won fame as a mining engineer. His mother Cecile, a skilled artist, drew the exquisite plates for her husband's treatise on fossil fishes. In 1845 Louis Agassiz came to America, leaving his wife, son and two daughters in Europe. In 1848, during the

Alexander Agassiz about 1860.

summer of which the elder Agassiz explored Lake Superior, Cecile died of tuberculosis. The following year the children joined their father in Massachusetts.

The younger Agassiz acquired his father's love of geology and natural history. He graduated from Harvard in 1855 and two years later earned another bachelor's degree in engineering and mining from the Lawrence Scientific School. Returning to Harvard to study chemistry, he received a third degree in natural history in 1862. In the meantime, in 1860 he had married Anna Russell, a member of one of the "Boston Brahmin" families.

In 1865, Agassiz temporarily applied his training in mining toward operating a coal mine in Pennsylvania. The following year he made two trips to the Keweenaw Peninsula to observe the workings of a pair of new copper mines, the Calumet and the Hecla (later amalgamated as the Calumet & Hecla) in which he had become interested.

A print of the interior of a copper mine, ca 1860.

Anna Russell Agassiz wore a revolver on her hip when she moved to the Keweenaw peninsula in 1867.

While most of the copper mines in the Keweenaw launched in the 1840s worked veins of pure native copper, the Calumet and Hecla lode consisted of hard copper-bearing conglomerate rock known as "pudding stone." Edwin J. Hulbert, a civil engineer, discovered the rich field in 1864. He shipped a barrel of the conglomerate to Boston to convince that city's wealthy speculators to invest in the mine. One such financial backer, Quincy A. Shaw, a cousin of historian Francis Parkman, was also a brother-in-law to young Agassiz.

Despite the potential of the conglomerate, the mine was making no money, in fact Calumet and Hecla operations swallowed up vast sums of Boston-backed finances with little to show. The major problem lay in the hardness of the conglomerate stone which could not be pulverized via the usual stamping process. Getting the ore 13 miles over the rugged Keweenaw terrain to the closest stamping mill ate up profits as well.

Shaw dispatched Agassiz to the Keweenaw to investigate the problem. The blame, he reported back, lay largely in

Hulbert's faulty planning and management. Accordingly, Shaw, who was now majority stockholder in the mine, appointed Agassiz superintendent to replace Hulbert in March, 1867. Hulbert ultimately lost all of his stake in the Calumet and Hecla and despite Shaw's generosity in placing him on a pension, he remained bitter for the rest of his life. He died in Italy in 1910 not long after, at the age of 65, he married 23-year-old Carla Caruso.

Before he left Boston for the Keweenaw, Agassiz met a young professor, Charles W. Eliot, who later became president of Harvard. He revealed his motive for moving to what was then Ultima Thule: "Eliot, I am going to Michigan for some years as superintendent of the Calumet and Hecla Mines. I want to make some money; it is impossible to be a productive naturalist in this country without money. I am going to get some money if I can and then I will be a naturalist." Because of that decision, years later Agassiz would become "the wealthiest professional zoologist who ever lived."

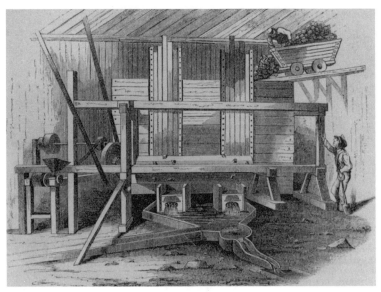

A primitive copper stamping mill, ca. 1860, could not handle the hard Calumet & Hecla ore.

Agassiz, his two young children and pretty wife, who walked around the Keweenaw frontier with a pistol strapped to her hip, spent two miserable, albeit productive, years in the Upper Peninsula. He worked 16, 18 sometimes 24 hours a day righting the operations. He believed firmly in spending as much money as it took to bring quality and that investment would pay off big in the long run. He sank shafts to convert the open pit operations into genuine mines to get at the rich copper lode. He constructed a railroad to carry ore from the mines to the sophisticated stamping mill he erected on the shore of Torch Lake four miles south, and he constantly experimented with novel rock crushers, smelters and other machines to more efficiently expedite copper production.

Not everything worked as smoothly as he planned. The steam locomotive he ordered proved to be a different gauge than the existing ore cars and track he had already laid. Costly non-productive weeks passed while the rail was relaid and the axles of the cars shortened.

Some of the locals who resented Hulbert's dismissal attempted to sabotage operations and foment labor troubles. They cut a channel through the dam Agassiz had built to impound water for his new stamp mill, then got a sympathetic judge to issue an injunction to prevent repairs. Agassiz, however, had a crew working on the dam early the following morning and completed repairs before the injunction could be served.

Agassiz's hard work and planning paid off. In August, 1868, the mines produced a total of 325 tons of ingot copper. In December of the following year the Hecla Mine paid its first dividend of $5.00 a share. By 1872 the company was shipping 65.3% of all the copper coming from Michigan and fully 50% of all U.S. produced red metal. From 1869 to 1884 Calumet and Hecla shareholders earned $25 million on an investment of $1.2 million. Shaw and Agassiz owned more than 25% of the company shares which by 1884 brought in nearly $6 million a year in dividends at a time when laborers earned about one dollar a day.

The success of the Calumet and Hecla spurred the rise of communities including; Calumet, Red Jacket, Laurium,

The Calumet & Hecla Mining Company's Shaft No. 2 at Calumet, ca. 1900.

Tamarack and Centennial Heights. Entrepreneurs and the company itself erected stores, banks, schools and churches to accommodate the thousands of miners, timber men, railroad workers and others who flocked to the Keweenaw. Anna Agassiz helped found the first church and Methodist sunday school in Calumet when she arrived in 1867.

By 1910 the Calumet and Hecla had built ten schools near the mines and the smelter at Torch Lake. One, the Washington School, a 192-foot long sandstone structure was "said to be the largest and best schoolhouse in the state" in 1875. The company built a public Library in Calumet in 1898, an architectural gem replete with 24 bath tubs for miner's use in the basement. By 1913 the library shelves held over 35,000 volumes "in more than a score of languages." The company also laid out baseball diamonds and operated a bowling alley and an indoor swimming pool for employees.

In October, 1868, the Agassiz family left the Keweenaw, traveling to Europe for a much needed vacation. In 1871, Agassiz was named president of the Calumet and Hecla, a position he held until his death in 1910. Twice a year Agassiz dutiful returned to the Keweenaw for inspection of the mine and the quasi-company towns around it.

Under Agassiz's paternal management, employees were treated better than was common in the industry. But he tolerated no union activity. When some newly arrived Swedish and Finnish miners staged a strike in 1874, he wrote the superintendent of the mines:

> *We cannot be dictated to by anyone. The mine must stop if it stays closed forever.... We have always treated our men fairly and honestly, they have received higher wages than any other corporation... They spit in my face... Wages will be raised whenever we see fit and at no other time (if they don't like it they must go and get employment elsewhere).*

Running a multimillion dollar mining operation became more or less a sideline to the career as a naturalist which

This postcard view sent from Calumet in 1909 depicts miners ascending from the depths of a copper mine.

Agassiz's growing wealth allowed. By 1872 he had begun issuing the great work of his life, a zoological treatise on sea urchins. Five years later he published another classic monograph on starfishes.

In 1873, Agassiz was overwhelmed by a double tragedy. His beloved father died, and wife Anna caught pneumonia while attending her father-in-law during his sickness and she died eight days later. So crushed was he by the loss of the love of his life that he was never able to speak of her death, even to friends.

In 1874, he was named curator of the unfinished museum at Harvard founded by his father. He solicited large sums and devoted about $1 million of his own funds to the natural history museum he dedicated to his father's memory.

Agassiz spent the remainder of his life, endlessly cruising aboard government vessels studying coral reefs and marine fauna. Unfortunately, he seems to have inherited his father's antipathy for Charles Darwin's theories and he spent much of his energy in attempting to debunk Darwin's work on the formation of coral atolls. Nevertheless, the magnificently illustrated reports on his explorations remain classics in the field. Contemporary scientists credited his work with contributing most of what was known during his lifeline of the configuration of ocean beds, continental shelves and the Gulf Stream. All was made possible by red rock riches harvested from the Keweenaw Peninsula.

In September, 1923, thousands gathered at Agassiz Memorial Park in Red Jacket (now part of Calumet) for the dedication of a world class athletic field and the unveiling of the bronze statue of the scientist, mine superintendent and company president who did so much to benefit the growth of Michigan's Keweenaw Peninsula. ■

In 1910, the year of Agassiz's death, downtown Calumet looked like this on April 10th.

XIII

AS THE BISHOP SAW IT

J.B. Mauntel, Bishop Caspar Borgess's close friend and traveling companion, stood gazing out the front window of their hotel room in Galway, a port city in western Ireland. To the west lay Claddagh, a village inhabited by what the American tourists thought a "peculiar and primitive race of people."

Suddenly, Mauntel exclaimed, "My gracious! I did not know that they had Indians in this country."

He had formed his idea of what Indians looked like from his visit to Cross Village, north of Harbor Springs, within Bishop Borgess's diocese. The bishop ran to the window and, sure enough, he too observed, "that both men and women of Claddagh in Galway dress and appear exactly like Indians."

Irish Indians were but one of the many adventures Borgess experienced during a trip through Europe in 1877. He related his observations in a series of letters to his friend Father Edward Joos of Monroe. Both Joos and Borgess had been mentors and close friends to Father Francis O'Brien. Borgess, in fact, had donated $5,000 in seed money, which, allowed his protégé to establish Kalamazoo's first hospital in 1889, named in the bishop's honor.

Following Borgess's death in 1890, O'Brien had sought to further perpetuate his memory through a four volume series on the bishop's life and letters. The first volume, and the only one ever published, appeared in 1892 under the imprint of Pauly, Fuchs & Co. of Detroit. It was actually printed by the Kalamazoo Publishing Company.

Entitled *As the Bishop Saw It*, the 266-page volume, appropriately bound in purple cloth, contains Borgess's letters about his European trips as edited by O'Brien. The proceeds from the book, which sold well among Kalamazoo's Catholic families, went toward easing the hospital through its tough early years.

Born August 1, 1826, in the village of Addrup, near the town of Essen in the Duchy of Oldenburg, Germany, Borgess immigrated with his parents to America at the age of 12. The

Bishop Caspar Borgess in Detroit, ca. 1880.

family eventually settled in Cincinnati where Borgess attended St. Xavier's College. Having made up his mind to enter the priesthood, he completed his education at Mount St. Mary's Seminary.

Ordained in 1848, he first served as pastor in Columbus, Ohio. His heroic efforts in administering to the victims of the cholera epidemic which devastated that city in 1849 helped determine his future role as a hospital advocate.

In 1870, Borgess was appointed Bishop of the Diocese of Detroit, which then included all of the Lower Peninsula of Michigan. Seven years later came the opportunity to make a pilgrimage to the Vatican. Following an audience with Pope Pius IX, he toured Europe.

While much of the travel narrative edited by O'Brien is devoted to visits to cathedrals, catacombs, shrines and celebrated churchmen there is enough of secular interest to make it fascinating reading. The bishop's keen sense of humor frequently shines forth.

While visiting a village in France, for example, he described an experience common to many another tourist: "Our proficiency in the Flemish language was insufficient for us to enter into a brisk conversation with people, consequently, we shared the usual misfortune of being supposed of being deaf, and everybody addressing us believed it necessary to shout at us, and we were obliged to bow and smile graciously in response to this torture."

In Rome, he found "the guides are as bad as mosquitoes in our own country; if you shoo one away, half a dozen are ready to pounce on you!"

Borgess frequently compared European scenery to that of Michigan. Lake Geneva, Switzerland, he thought miniscule compared to Lake St. Clair. While traveling by train through France, he noted, "the soil from Bordeaux to Dax is evidently very poor, and it reminds us strongly of the northern portion of Michigan, along the railroad line north of Bay City, where the jack-pine flourishes, which also abounds here. But even the jack-pine is utilized by the economical French, every tree being tapped for resin, like the maple trees at home."

Father Francis O'Brien of Kalamazoo was a close friend of Bishop Borgess.

His most colorful descriptions, however, followed his arrival in Ireland. Upon reaching Dublin, he sadly noted: "In France, Italy, Germany and Switzerland intemperance on the streets is among the rare events, in Holland, Belgium and England it is met with from time to time, but here it is an exception if you do not meet it within every square."

In Belfast, Borgess found the entire city in revolt, with mobs of Catholics and Protestants battling each other. While passing through the lines of the belligerents, he experienced "some uneasiness" when after his carriage stopped he glanced out the window to find himself "surrounded by a thousand young women whose aprons were filled with boulders."

The morning after his arrival, Borgess and Mauntel took a stroll. Leaving the main artery, High Street, they meandered down narrow side roads seeking to develop a real feel for the city. Suddenly they found themselves in an out-of-the-way market. Fellow pedestrians glowered and "frowned in bitterness" at the black robed priest. They had blundered into the very heart

The Green Linen Market in Belfast, a Protestant stronghold that Bishop Borgess blundered into.

of "orange country," a district known as Shank's Hill. Luckily, the lost Americans found their way out of "the camp of the enemy" without being stoned.

Leaving that strife ridden city, Borgess paid an obligatory visit to Blarney Castle where he kissed the Blarney Stone. Soon thereafter he boarded the steamer *City of Berlin* and embarked for his beloved Michigan.

Back in Detroit, Borgess continued to cater to the increasing needs of the European immigrants flocking to find jobs amid the city's burgeoning industrial growth. Of the ten new parishes organized during his leadership, eight were foreign-language speaking, including Bohemian, German, French, Polish and Belgian.

Borgess retired in 1887 and purchased a home near Lake St. Clair in Grosse Pointe. During a visit to Father O'Brien, in Kalamazoo, Borgess suffered an attack of apoplexy and died a week later. His remains were temporarily buried in St. Augustine's churchyard. In 1906 they were placed in a tomb on the grounds of Nazareth Academy, at the northeastern Kalamazoo city limits, where an imposing marble shaft was erected in his memory.

The hospital that bears his name continues as a vibrant Kalamazoo institution. Sadly, the troubles he witnessed in Ireland in 1877 would continue for more than a century. ■

Borgess Hospital, funded through a gift of Bishop Borgess, opened in a converted Kalamazoo home in 1889.

XIV

JOHNSTON'S GOT YOUR BIBLE

"Throughout his long life, Theron Johnston never forgot that summer's day in 1877. What had drawn the 15-year-old from his home in Allegan County's Casco Township, just north of South Haven, a half dozen miles east to Lee Township, he failed to record. He may have been hunting the rabbits, wild turkey and other game animals that abounded in the township's sandy cut-over plains. Or the ambrosial thumb-sized blackberries that festooned the big white pine stumps might have lured him there.

But the highlight of his day's wanderings, the discovery of an old, seemingly abandoned, log cabin in Section 18 of the township, became an indelible memory. Upon entering, among the litter of household paraphernalia he spied an old, worn, leather-bound volume. The lengthy title, beginning with "Kekitchemanitomenahn," seemed of incomprehensible gibberish save for one name in English, "Jesus Christ," and the imprint, Albany, 1833. Johnston held in his hands a copy of the New Testament translated into the Algonquian Indian language by Edwin James, best known for ghost writing the autobiography of John Tanner, the "Wild Man of Sault Ste. Marie," who had been kidnapped and raised by the Indians.

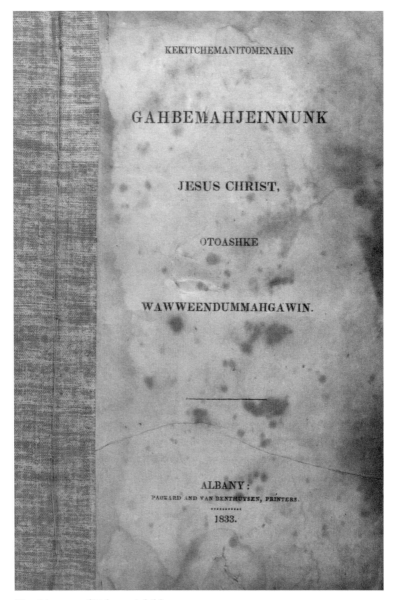

The title page of Pokagon's bible.

To whom the cabin and its contents rightly belonged Johnston never admitted knowing. But this he did acknowledge to his dying day - he took the Indian Bible.

Actually, the ownership of the cabin and its contents might have been easily determined by consulting the *Allegan County Atlas* published in 1873. There, clearly outlined and identified in Section 18, lies the 40-acre tract owned by Simon Pokagon, the most celebrated Michigan Indian of the last half of the 19th Century.

He was the son of Chief Leopold Pokagon, a legendary Potawatomi statesman whose sagacity in allotting treaty payments toward purchasing property for the people of his band had prevented them from being rounded up and herded across the Mississippi River at bayonet point in 1840, like most other Michigan Potawatomi. Born in 1825 or 1830, sources vary, at a sugar camp near the present site of Pokagon in Cass County, Simon spent his youth in an ancient Potawatomi village on the St. Joseph River in southern Berrien County.

Until he was 12-years-old, he knew only his native Algonquian tongue. As a young adult and ambitious to better his and his people's lot, he managed to gain admittance to Notre Dame where he studied for four or five years. Then he spent a year at Oberlin College and two years at the Indian academy at Twinsburg, Ohio. Initially trained for the priesthood, he ultimately abandoned that vocation but not before mastering four languages. He gained the reputation as "the best educated full-blooded Indian of his time."

Pokagon spent many a summer vacation hunting and fishing with his mother, the sister of the illustrious Chief Topinabee, and a compassionate French fur trader, Joseph Bertrand, while roaming the land of the Ottawa in Van Buren and Allegan counties. During one such sojourn in the wilderness, he met a beautiful maiden named Lonidaw Sinagaw. They fell in love and married. Lonidaw bore four children but, tragically, died in 1871 at the age of 35.

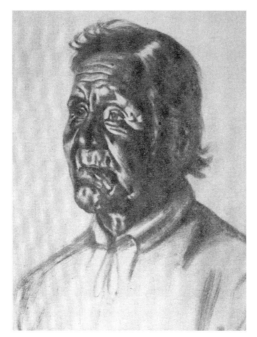

Chicago artist E. A. Burbank painted the kindly Pokagon in 1898, just months before his death.

Pokagan raised the small children himself. Family grief persisted - only one son survived his father.

Decades later, Julia Pokagon Quingo remembered her grandfather as a kind and cheerful man who dearly loved children. Wherever he went a crowd of youngsters trailed behind. Others recall Pokagon talking to wild birds and animals in Algonquian or poring over books in "strange tongues." Like his father, he embraced the Catholic faith and remained deeply religious throughout his life, often assisting the priests in interpreting their teachings to his people.

Washington Engle, a young attorney from Hartford, remembered getting lost in the forest and stumbling upon Pokagon's cabin. He knocked at the door and was startled to be greeted by a tall Indian holding open a testament which at a glance appeared to be written in Greek - or was it the 1833 Bible in Algonquian?

Engel and Pokagon became fast friends over the succeeding 40 years, and the lawyer provided him *pro bono* advice. The legal services required by Pokagon related to his decades-long campaign to secure payment to his people, as promised in the treaty his father had signed in 1833 that ceded more than one million acres of ancestral land to the federal government, including the site of Chicago. Pokagon journeyed to Washington for an interview with President Ulysses Grant in 1870s to no avail. Petitions he delivered were repeatedly tied up in congressional committees. He may well have been off on some such mission when Johnston got his Bible

The national spotlight focused on Pokagon in 1893 through his activities during the Columbian Exposition, an epic world's fair held in Chicago to commemorate the 400th anniversary of the "discovery" of American. When Pokagon visited the fair shortly after its opening, he

A rare copy of the fragile birch-bark book Pokagon sold at the Columbian Exposition in 1893.

discerned nothing to commemorate the story of the nation's original inhabitants. He penned a well written essay, "Red Man's Rebuke," a touching lament over the demise of his people, printed it as a pamphlet on birch bark and hawked it at the fair. When Chicago Mayor Carter Harrison read the piece, he invited Pokagon to deliver an address before an estimated 750,000 visitors who thronged the exhibition during Chicago Day, October 9, 1893.

About the time Pokagon was enjoying the height of his fame, Theron Johnston's varied career had also taken an upswing. After moving with his family as a three-year-old from Indiana to Casco Township in 1864, Johnston spent his youth and early manhood engaged in the backbreaking labor of converting virgin wilderness into the 160-acre family farm. His book learning ended with graduation from the eighth grade in a nearby one room schoolhouse. For several years he plied the carpenter's trade and worked briefly at an area hospital. He saved his small earnings, and in 1893, in partnership with his brother, Adelbert, he purchased a general store in the little Casco Township community that had grown up around the flour mill established by William Hawkhead.

The following year he bought out his brother and took as his business and marriage partner, Rose Bugden. The family soon included three children. Johnston also became the Hawkhead postmaster with the post office allotted a corner of the store.

In the meantime, Pokagon had continued to garner literary honors throughout the 1890s. He published a variety of articles on Indian lore and handiwork in *Harper's Monthly*, *The Arena*, *Chautauquan* and other popular journals of the time, four additional birch bark pamphlets and a number of poems and songs lyrics. The press dubbed him "the Longfellow of his race."

Pokagon also became a popular orator, delivering poignant addresses at historical celebrations and

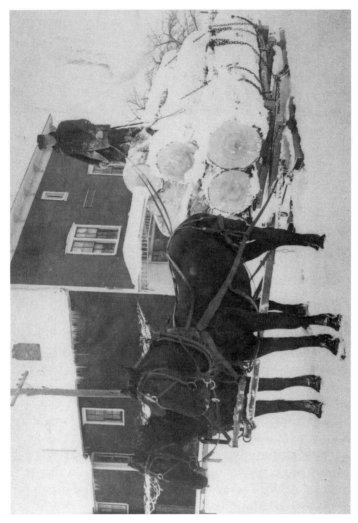

In 1913, the camera captured a load of massive maple logs in front of Theron Johnston's Hawkhead general store.

elsewhere. Due, in part, to the publicity he engendered, the federal government finally awarded the Potawatomi the tribe's long-due treaty payments in 1895. On August 25, 1897, Pokagon gave a stirring speech at the semi-centennial celebration of the founding of Holland, Michigan. He told the surviving Dutch pioneers who had pushed the resident Ottawa off their ancient domain:

> *The same forest that frowned on you smiled upon us, the same forest that was ague and death to you, was our bulwark and defense. The same forest you have cut down and destroyed, we loved and our great fear was, that the White man in his advance westward would mar or destroy it.*
>
> *I am getting old and feeble, and feel that one foot is lifted to step into the world beyond. I have stood all my life as a peacemaker between your people and my people, trying to sooth the prejudices of the two races toward each other. Yes, without bow or gun I have stood as one standing between two armies advancing toward each other for the fight, receiving a thousand wounds from your people and my own people.*

In late 1898, friend Engle was assisting him in publishing the chief's *magnum opus*, a semi-autobiographical novel titled *Queen of the Woods*. Amidst the throes of completing a book, Pokagon's primary residence burned to the ground, taking with it the manuscripts and mementos of his life's work. Penniless and devastated by the loss, the old man grew weaker and weaker. He took his last refuge in the tumble-down log cabin in Lee Township, and on January 27, 1899, he died there of pneumonia. Whatever comfort the dying Indian may have derived from reading the Lord's Prayer in his native

Pokagon's semi-autobiographical novel published following his death in 1899.

tongue can only be surmised - because Johnston had his Bible.

A few weeks later, Engle released the first edition of *Queen of the Woods*. The book that Pokagon had never seen, arguably the first such work to be written by a pure blooded American Indian, became a minor classic, going through at least seven editions. In his final days Pokagon had expressed a wish to be buried next to Lonidaw's grave in the cemetery at the old Indian church on the

Pokagon's grave lies near the St. Dominic Church at Rush Lake.

south shore of Rush Lake in southern Van Buren County. Because Pokagon's second wife had been a divorced woman it took a special dispensation for him to be buried in the consecrated cemetery. On the day of his funeral, the Indians in attendance waited for more than an hour for the arrival of a priest. When he finally appeared, Pokagon had already been buried in an unmarked grave without benefit of the last sacred rites. Nearby, a copse of trees marks the graves of his four children.

The year of Pokagon's death brought a turning point in the destiny of Johnston and his Hawkhead community as well. From a high of 100 that year the population steadily decreased. In 1902, Johnston lost his job as postmaster when the office shifted to nearby Kibbie. As fewer and fewer customers entered the store, Johnston sold it in 1920.

On January 1st, 1926, Johnston presented the old Indian Bible to the South Haven City Library, with an appended page documenting his version of its provenance. Thirteen years later, Johnston, then nearing 80-years of age, asked for its return. A. B. Chase, president of the library board, honored that request. Following Johnston's death, the battered artifact bounced around to various antique shops and old book stores.

The veteran volume survives, testament to a disgraceful chapter in Anglo/Indian relations when nothing the native American had, even his Bible, lay beyond the white man's grasp.

But, then again, maybe old Chief Pokagon got the last laugh - Johnston's long abandoned store was demolished in 1968, and Hawkhead is a ghost town. ■

XV

Autumn Ramblings in Northern Michigan

A pristine Michigan morning greeted George Oliver Shields and four companion sportsmen as they clambered down from the Grand Rapids and Indiana Railroad car at Elmira, a little station 25 miles south of Petoskey. The quintet had traveled by rail nearly 600 miles from Louisville, Kentucky, intent on enjoying an invigorating week of deer hunting in the northern Michigan wilds. It was September 4, 1878.

Two factors, however, stood in the way of their success. In 1859, Michigan's first state-wide act for the protection of wildlife had prohibited the killing of deer from January through July. Another act in 1873 limited the hunting period from October 1 to December 31. So the Kentucky sportsmen were hunting out of season. They were in good company. Hunters paid scant attention to these irritating laws because there were no game wardens. Not until 1887 would William Alden Smith be appointed the state's one and only game warden. In the meantime, few sheriffs or other local law officials risked antagonizing voters over unpopular game enforcement.

Potentially a conscientious citizen could seek prosecution of violators - but that rarely happened. On a June morning in

1881, a wealthy lumberman from Saginaw, William B. Mershon, observed two men hauling a freshly killed deer. He persuaded the local prosecutor to take on the case, and during a short trial the men were proven guilty. Whereupon the jury of local peers delivered the verdict, "Not Guilty." When questioned, the jurors responded, "He didn't prove it was a wild deer - it might have been tame."

The Kentucky hunters learned of the other adverse factor they faced when after a 40-mile wagon ride over rough roads they reached their camp site on one of the Twin Lakes in the southwestern tip of Montmorency County. An old hunter informed them that there was scarcely a chance of getting any deer because:

> *At this particular season the does were weaning their fawns and were lying hidden away from them all through the day; that the fawns being naturally the most timid creatures in the wild, would not venture out to feed during the day alone; that the bucks were also lying hidden away drying their horns, and that each ventured out to feed only at night.*

If they had only chosen a time a few weeks earlier or later, they would have had no trouble getting plenty of easy shots. The disappointed sportsmen resolved to make the best of the situation and hired the old hunter to guide them, hoping to get at least enough venison to eat during their stay.

The next morning they set out single file through the dense forest of great Norway pine, some trees five and six feet in diameter. They entered a jack-pine plain, where fire had burned the old growth, allowing young trees and brush to flourish, forming near perfect deer browse. Suddenly a magnificent buck leaped from his hiding place. The guide, in front, aimed and squeezed the trigger, but his rifle misfired. The others couldn't get a shot without hitting the guide until the deer bounded slightly out of line and Shields snap shot a bullet flying past the

Shields flagging antelopes out west. The animals will approach anything that piques their curiosity.

guide but missed the buck. That was the last deer they saw that day.

Shields recorded his hunting adventures in a chapter, "Autumn Ramblings in Northern Michigan," part of his 1883 book, *Rustlings in the Rockies*. The 306-page volume documents his adventures while killing just about every animal he encountered in the Rockies, Great Plains, Florida and Wisconsin. Most often he slew simply for the pleasure of it. Out west he shot countless buffalo, elk, and mule deer. He and a comrade flagged in a herd of curious antelope, and a minute later five of them lay dead. Shields tracked down a grizzly bear with two cubs and blew gaping holes in all three with the 40-caliber "explosive bullets" he preferred and harvested only their claws as souvenirs.

In Florida, he sniped huge sunning alligators from a boat as well as every blue heron, white egret and blue ibis he saw. In Wisconsin he prided himself on his skill in shooting loons.

Born in Batavia, Ohio, in 1846, Shields, proud to be an autodidact, received only three months of formal education before the family immigrated to Iowa. At the age of eighteen he enlisted in the Union Army and three months later took a bullet in the Battle of Resaca, Georgia. After the war he drifted west and began writing for newspapers and magazines. He collected a series of those articles in book form for *Rustlings In the Rockies*, *Cruising in the Cascades* (1889) and a half dozen other volumes about hunting, fishing, camping, big game, Native Americans and a classic book on dogs.

A nimrod of Shield's experience should have researched the deer hunting situation in Northern Michigan before traveling 600 miles. But, evidently, he had not, and in September, 1878, the sportsmen were hunting out of season with the deer in hiding. They spent the week fishing, landing a 30-inch pickerel and a number of four-pound black bass, and while fruitlessly seeking deer succeeded in getting lost in the deep woods several times. During one such blunder, Shields managed to stumble upon a German homesteader's cabin and spent the night there. Another misadventure found the whole party forced to curl up on the ground in the woods before a blazing campfire while being serenaded by a wolf pack.

The results of the flagging - less than 60 seconds of shooting. Shields later campaigned to prevent the extinction of antelope.

When a pair of the Kentuckians went fishing in a rowboat, a big, black bear lumbered to the lake shore and stood on his hind legs to get a better look at the humans. Of course they fired at it, putting a bullet through its haunches and after a brief unsuccessful search, left the poor animal to suffer a slow death.

At the week's end, the luckless hunters broke camp, loaded their luggage on the wagon that had returned for them and jolted back along the tote road running from the railroad station to scattered lumber camps in the region. They stopped for the night at the driver's home, a few miles from Elmira. There, they heard the baying of a hound in the woods, and shortly after a deer bounded across the field and into a nearby small lake. The hunters grabbed their weapons and raced to different points on the lake. One, armed with a Smith & Wesson revolver, put a bullet in the swimming deer's head. It proved to be a fawn, whose tender meat the hunters enjoyed during the remainder of the trip.

Setting aside it being out of season, this method of deer hunting was perfectly legal at the time. Not until 1881 would the Michigan legislature prohibit taking deer in the water and killing fawns. That act also made it illegal to ship deer out of state in an effort to curtail the professional market hunters who had killed 100,000 Michigan deer in 1880 alone.

In 1887, Michigan first outlawed hunting deer with hounds and shining them at night. When the anti-dog regulation went into effect, a famous hunting club of wealthy sportsmen on the Au Sable River disbanded because they thought hunting without hounds would not be fun anymore. The first bag limit of five deer came in 1895. Within 20 years, as the game grew increasingly scarce, the limit was reduced to one deer each season.

The morning after they had shot the fawn, the sportsmen ate an early breakfast and were driven to Elmira where they took the train to Petoskey. There they switched trains for Lakeview at the head of Crooked Lake and boarded the little steamer *Northern Belle* for the forty-four mile trip to Cheboygan via Crooked, Burt, Mullett lakes and connecting waterways. Enroute, "several ducks were taught the folly of exposing themselves to the unerring aim of some of our crack shots." The sportsmen amused themselves by plinking divers and wood ducks on the wing as well as several other species as they sat in the water. The dead ducks bobbed in the wake of the vessel, retrieval not even attempted.

At Cheboygan the party boarded the steamer *Mary* for Mackinac Island where the Kentuckians spent several days before returning south.

Like many another old hunter with satiated blood lust, by the 1890s Shields had evolved into a genuine sportsman - and a conservationist. In 1894, he founded the popular journal

A camp of northern Michigan deer hunters, ca. 1880.

Recreation, and in its pages he waged vigorous campaigns against the excessive killing of game and later the use of automatic shotguns. About 1901, he began crusading for a temporary ban on hunting antelope, then close to extinction.

    From 1897 to 1902 he headed up the conservationist Campfire Club of America. He founded the League of American Sportsmen in 1898 which successfully promoted the appointment of game wardens in a number of states as well as the encouragement of animal photography rather than killing. By August, 1912, Shields devoted most of his energies to lecturing and was influential in getting game laws enacted in numerous states. The man who was called by the editor of *Outdoor Life* "unquestionably our most eminent and successful pioneer in the cause of the conservation of wild life" died penniless in New York City in 1925, having devoted all his fortune toward the cessation of the merciless slaughter of animals that he had once so avidly enjoyed.■

XVI

BIG HEADS & BUMP BUNKUM

Samuel Bickley, Jr., an itinerant phrenologist who had journeyed from New York to read the heads of Flint citizens in 1881, pursed his lips as he scanned the number on the measuring tape next to his thumbnail. At a full 23¾ inches in circumference, Mary Johnson's head was enormous - it rated a full "7," the highest ranking in the phrenological scale. Hers was among the largest woman's head he'd ever had the honor to do.

A practitioner of the flim-flam belief that analysis of the size and shape of the head and facial features as well as a series of bumps on the skull identifying character traits could reveal the personality and potential for success of a subject, Bickley knew that a big head meant a correspondingly large brain. "That size is a measure of power, is a universal law" was fully elucidated in the *New Illustrated Self-Instructor in Phrenology*, a 176 page manual replete with more than 100 depictions of representative heads, good ones and bad, which Bickley hawked to his audiences.

Chapter Nine of the volume laid out the proof:

> *All really great men have great heads - merely smart ones, not always. The brains of Cuvier (naturalist), Byron (poet) and Spurzheim (pioneer phrenologist) were among the heaviest ever*

weighed. True, Byron's hat was small, doubtless because his brain was conical; and most developed in the base; but its great weight establishes its great size. So does that of (Napoleon) Bonaparte. Besides he wore a very large hat - one that passed clear over the head of Col. Lehmenouski, one of his body guard, whose head measured 23½ inches. Webster's head was massive, measuring over 24 inches, and Clay's 23½; and this is about Van Buren's size... Hamilton's

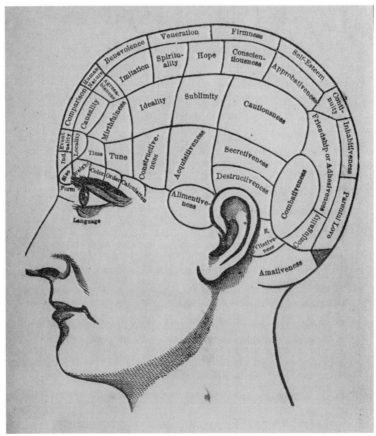

The phrenological "organs" fully mapped out.

hat passed over the head of a man whose head measured 23½. Burke's (British statesman) head was immense, so was Jefferson's, while Franklin's hat passed over the ears of a 24 - inch head. The heads of Washington, Adams, and a thousand other celebrities, were also very large.

What motivated those distinguished personages to try on each other's hats and who took the liberty of weighing their brains, hopefully *post mortem*, remains an enigma.

To return to Flint of 1881, where Bickley's expert hands made their way across Mary Johnson's scalp, pausing only to quickly rate on a chart the 37 discrete "organs" early phrenologists had mapped out on the human skull. He graded her a "6" for conjugality (marriage), friendship, cautiousness, benevolence and constructiveness. She slipped down to "5's" in combativeness, acquisitiveness, secretiveness and spirituality. She zoomed up to a "7" in parental love, as any good mother should, but only managed "4's" in language and continuity. Bickley paused as he rubbed the organ of amativeness at the base of her skull, and then jotted down a healthy "6" for what we would now term sexuality.

Finished with Mary, Bickley tackled her husband, W.J.C. Johnson, an English immigrant who operated a tailor shop on Kearsley Street. The phrenologist involuntarily shook his head as he read the tape. The tailor's noggin measured a full ½ inch smaller than his wife's, whereas the average woman's head ran about an inch smaller than a man's. Moving on to the cranial manipulation, Bickley rated most of the organs "5" or "6," amativeness got a full "6." But "time" and unfortunately "agreeableness" yielded only "4s." Despite Bickley's somewhat negative ratings of the Johnson's matrimonial compatibility, based on a flyleaf annotation on the couple's long cherished copy of the *Self Instructor in Phrenology*, happily, the marriage of the grumpy tailor and big headed woman survived.

Nineteenth Century Americans moved in a yeasty ferment of avant-garde movements geared toward ameliorating society's

AVERAGE MEASUREMENT
WITH CALLIPERS,
For a Well Balanced Head

J. C. Johnson — *Wife*

23 1/4 Circumference Around Head with Tape, 21½ inches. **23 3/4**

8	Individuality to Philoprogenitiveness,	7 6 inches.	**8.4**
5.2	Ear to Individuality, ...	4 6 inches.	**5.5**
5.3	Ear to Philoprogenitiveness, ...	4 5 inches.	**5.3**
6.4	Ear to Firmness, ...	5 6 inches.	**6.1**
6.2	Ear to Benevolence, ...	5 5 inches.	**6.2**
6.5	Destructiveness to Destructiveness,	6 inches.	**6.6**
6.4	Cautiousness to Cautiousness, ...	5 6 inches.	**6.6**
5.4	Ideality to Ideality, ...	5 3 inches.	**5.5**
6	Ear to Self-Esteem, ...	5 5 inches.	**6**
6	Ear to Comparison, ...	5 3 inches.	**6**

A CHART
OF THE CHARACTER AND NATURAL TALENTS OF

Mr. J. C. Johnson and Wife

AS GIVEN BY

SAMUEL BICKLEY, JR.,
Practical Phrenologist.

Part of the phrenological chart compiled by Bickley on the Johnsons in Flint in 1881.

many woes. Temperance reformers, abolitionists, spiritualists, Mormon elders, Seventh-Day Adventist vegetarians, Bloomers and Graham cracker zealots thundered from the nation's rostrums. The apostle of yet another panacea, phrenology, crossed the Atlantic from Germany in June, 1832. Dr. Johann Gaspar Spurzheim, a disciple of the Viennese physician, Franz Joseph Gall, who had originated phrenology when he noticed his classmates with "good memories had large foreheads," delivered a series of popular lectures on the science in Boston.

Despite Spurzheim's sad demise two short months after his arrival in America (his brain was pickled and placed on exhibit at Harvard Medical School), his learned lectures inspired an epidemic acceptance of the novel theory. British tourist Harriet Martineau observed that "when Spurzheim was in America, the great mass of society became phrenologists in a day, wherever he appeared, … all caps and wigs… (were) pulled off, and all fair tresses disheveled, in search after organization."

By the 1850s, the New York publishing firm founded by Samuel Wells and brothers Lorenzo and Orson Fowler (best known for his sex manuals and invention of the octagon house style) had emerged as the nation's leading proponent of phrenology. Fowler and Wells broadcast million of copies of books on the subject as well as plaster of Paris heads with the 37 zones clearly delineated. Affiliated with the firm was Nelson Sizer, a celebrated phrenologist credited with reading more than 300,000 heads over his 40-year career.

Into Sizer's New York office on May 18, 1874, strode a "quiet gentleman in plain, citizen's dress," requesting a full phrenological reading. Sizer measured his head at 23 inches and told him he needed to gain about 15 pounds to put his body in alliance with his head size. After feeling up his bumps, he dictated his analysis that basically branded him as impetuous, headstrong and with a tendency to overdo any task at hand. "If you were an army officer and in active service, you would get as much work out of a horse as General Custer or Phil Sheridan would, that is to say, as much as the horse could render," Sizer admonished.

At the end of the session, to Sizer's surprise, the stranger revealed himself to be none other than George Armstrong Custer, himself, having shorn his famous flowing locks to attend close friend Gen. Philip Sheridan's wedding in Chicago. Thirteen months later, on June 25, 1876, Custer's impetuosity, arrogance and furious energy cost the lives of he and his command at the Little Big Horn. Sizer considered that deplorable outcome as ample vindication of the accuracy of his headwork on the cavalryman whose heroic bronze statue stands in his boyhood home of Monroe, Michigan.

George Armstrong Custer had his red-head read in 1875.

In 1865, another Michigander, and one who would make his mark in the bump bunco circuit, Thomas Sheldon Andrews, had his head read by the master phrenologist, Orson S. Fowler, himself. Born in 1829 near Detroit, Andrews had led a colorful life as a cabin boy on Great Lakes steamships, hotel manager in the Keweenaw Peninsula, and pioneer farmer in Kansas during the turbulent "Bleeding Kansas" era of the 1850s. Following Fowler's head session he decided to pursue that potentially lucrative endeavor himself.

After several bumpy marriages to women whose cranial development did not measure up to his own, he found his true love in a corpulent lady named Annie. Soon "Dr." and Mrs. Dr. Andrews displayed their physiognomic (another name for phrenology) skills before audiences across Michigan and the Midwest. During the 1860s-1880s the pair specialized in predicting the compatibility of prospective marriage partners based on the couple's head sizes and, of course, matching bumps.

Charles E. Weller, the son of a Swedenborgian minister, grew up in Grand Rapids in the 1850s. In his autobiography he documented the visit to that frontier town on the Grand River by another unnamed phrenologist. The "professor's" arrival was heralded for weeks in advance by a series of large posters depicting a head mapped out with the phrenological zones. Upon alighting from the stagecoach that carried him from Kalamazoo, the closest railroad depot, the "head master" proceeded to deliver two weeks of free evening lectures to culture-starved Grand Rapidians.

Having whetted their interest in the marvelous science, he offered personal readings in his hotel room during the day. Parents of promising boys, in particular, flocked to the professor's room. Whatever their head size, he gratified all expectations with "bright prospects for a future career which may even lead to the presidency of the United States." At two dollars a head and averaging 25-30 readings a day, the phrenologist netted during his two weeks more than the average yearly wage of local laborers.

The Eagle Hotel, where the quack phrenologist duped Grand Rapidians for two weeks in the 1850's.

But the professor's spiel did not gull all the "local yokels." To quiet the growing criticisms of these "doubting Thomases," the phrenologist proposed that he be tested by a blindfold reading of the head of someone selected by a committee of citizens. After properly "hoodwinking" the professor, the committee led his subject to the stage, a mental defective known around town as "Crazy Mary."

The professor ran his highly sensitive hands over the women's head and soon pronounced her "a lady of most remarkably strong character and possessing unusual talents in music, art and literature, as a leader in society." When relieved of his blindfold and made aware of the true nature of Mary, he simply responded that "she would have possessed precisely the qualities stated, had she not unfortunately lost her mind."

The professor, himself, lost little time in departing Grand Rapids early the next morning. Young Weller noticed that those who had paid to have their charts compiled by the quack "did not seem to set so high a value on them as they did at the outset."

Despite periodic unmasking of phrenological charlatans, the discipline retained a bevy of stalwart advocates throughout the Nineteenth Century, many of them seemingly intelligent men and women. None other than Woodbridge N. Ferris, founder of the Big Rapids university that bears his name and who served as governor of Michigan in 1913-1917, credited a good deal of his success to a firm belief in phrenology. "Through the reading of Fowler I was ushered into a new world," he wrote in 1921.

By the time of Ferris's testimonial, phrenology had pretty much run its course, succeeded by various fads, follies and frauds of the Twentieth Century ranging from Freudian psychology, handwriting analysis and Scientology to implanted goat gonads, alcohol-laden Hadacol and Wall Street bunco. Yet remnants remain in the 21st Century. What is criminal profiling if not a glorified version of phrenology? So next time you are waiting in line at the airport - heads up! ∎

XVII

SHANTY BOYS OF THE NORTH WOODS

John W. Fitzmaurice long remembered the miserable trek he endured while trudging 14 miles over a wilderness "tote road" to the remote lumber camp about ten miles southwest of Hubbard Lake in Algonac County. It was the winter of 1883 and 18 inches of newly fallen snow covered the trackless path. Without snowshoes, he stumbled, bone weary, into the camp about seven in the evening.

As was the custom, the crew of thirty "shanty boys" welcomed the stranger into the bunk house, heated by a roaring cast iron stove. Fitzmaurice was a hospital agent seeking to sell the men "hospital tickets" which entitled them to unlimited use of a Bay City Hospital should they became injured in the course of their hazardous occupation. To supplement the small percentage he retained of each of the policies which cost the insured only nine cents a week, he had invested in $600 worth of gold watches and jewelry he hoped to hawk as well.

He laid out his entire stock for examination and watched with a sinking feeling when a huge lumberman, the "camp hustler," took possession of the entire lot and proceeded to divide it into 30 little piles arranged along the bench that encircled the room. An accomplice called out the names of each of the men who promptly appropriated one of the allotments, "and at once proceeded to examine it piece by piece, with a childish curiosity." Fitzmaurice had just been looted of

This typical northern Michigan lumber camp located on Sand Creek near Whitehall in Muskegon County was painted by Frederick Norman in the late 19th Century. (Courtesy Whitehall Office Muskegon Bank & Trust Co.)

jewelry worth about $25,000 in modern equivalence and there was nothing he could do about it. To add insult to injury, he was told to "bunk in" with the burley pirate who had instigated the plundering.

Fitzmaurice recorded that experience and many another adventure in northern Michigan lumber camps of the 1880s in his classic account, *"The Shanty Boy," or Life In a Lumber Camp*, published in Cheboygan in 1889. Printed in a small edition with paper covers and mostly read to pieces by the lumberjacks who were the intended audience, the original volumes have become rare and valuable collector's items. More importantly, the volume contains the single best description of the heyday of Michigan lumbering at a time when the state led the nation in annual production.

Born on Cape Breton Island in the Gulf of St. Lawrence in 1833, Fitzmaurice moved with his family to Niagara, Ontario, three years later. At the age of 15 he joined the Royal Navy, serving off the coast of Africa while combating the slave trade. He left the service when he was 18 and moved to Buffalo, New York, where he worked in the iron industry. A year later a fiery blast from the furnace scorched the hair off his head, and it never grew back.

The bald youth became enamored with the Congregational Church, and in 1865 he was ordained a minister in Bedford, Calhoun County. After preaching in several Michigan communities he abandoned the active ministry because of the poor financial rewards. In 1870 he settled for a while in East Saginaw and began writing for several local newspapers. He soon developed a lively journalistic style, but, like many another wordsmith, he fell under the sway of liquor.

In 1876, Fitzmaurice realized he had become an alcoholic. He took "the pledge" that year and launched yet another career as a temperance lecturer, admonishing crowds across Michigan, Ohio and Ontario. He once spoke 138 nights in succession in Toronto and Hamilton, Ontario, convincing thousands to embrace the "red ribbon" symbol of the movement, which four decades later culminated in National Prohibition for America.

By 1880 his overly passionate pursuit of the calling had weakened his constitution and shrunken his normally muscular build by forty pounds. To regain his health a Bay City physician convinced Fitzmaurice to try a winter in the woods working for him as a hospital agent among the "red sash brigade." There was a genuine need for hospitals catering to lumbermen at that time. The winter of 1884-1885, alone, brought more than 3,000 accidents in the woods from toppling trees, dead branches that fell without warning called "widow makers" and limbs crushed between logs on the river. The mayhem killed 60 shanty boys, severely injured another 3,000, and that many more suffered disabling sickness. During the 1870s and 1880s Catholic sisters and medical entrepreneurs established "woodsmen's hospitals" in Saginaw, Bay City, Big Rapids, Flint, Grand Rapids, Alpena, Oscoda, Marquette and other lumbering communities of the north.

One crisp morning in November, 1880, Fitzmaurice boarded a Michigan Central Railroad train bound for Roscommon and the start of his new adventurous career. He had adopted the uniform of the other numerous shanty boys aboard, "good, warm, woolen pants, known as 'Canadian gray,' blue woolen shirt, German socks, walking rubbers strapped about the ankle, French head covering of the variegated night cap persuasion, and a heavy overcoat." Like the others he also sported the badge of the woodsman, a red sash wrapped around his waist.

The hospital agent's wardrobe echoed the various nationalities of the rough and tumble lumbermen on the train - French, German, Swedish, Irish, English, Polish and native American. He found the railroad car filled with "drunken, swearing, sweltering humanity, hilariously noisy" and busy passing bottles of the "budge" which was forbidden once they reached the lumber camps.

Fitzmaurice put up for the night at a Roscommon hotel, "swarming with recruits for the great army of the pine." Lodged in a small room containing three beds occupied by himself and five drunken, snoring woodsmen, the hospital agent spent a

Michigan lumberjacks making "light in the swamp," ca. 1880.

"hideous" night, enlivened also by an infestation of what the shanty boys termed "Michigan crumbs," big gray-backed bed bugs. Early the next morning, following a hurried breakfast, Fitzmaurice and his companions of the night before, slung their "turkeys" or clothes bags over their shoulders and set out on a twenty mile hike along a "tote road" to the lumber camp.

Later in his narrative, Fitzmaurice described a typical lumber camp on the Ocqueoc River west of Rogers City in Presque Isle County. Freshly built for one winter's work in getting out ten million board feet of timber, the camp consisted of a 65-foot-long cook and dining hall, a bunk house of 60 x 30 feet capable of sleeping 100 men, a barn and stable for 18 teams of horses and a blacksmith shop where all the tools, sleighs, etc. were made and repaired. During the six months spent in the woods the 100 shanty boys consumed each week: six - 60 pound barrels of flour, two and half big barrels of pickled beef, two and a half barrels of salted pork, eight bushels of potatoes, three bushels of onions, 15 pounds of pickles, a barrel of sugar, 25 pounds of tea, 16 pounds of coffee, 50 pounds of butter and 40 pounds of good, old-fashioned, stick-to-the-ribs lard.

As Fitzmaurice found out during his eight year tenure working among the shanty boys, a successful lumber camp needed two requisites, a good cook and a good fiddler. "All else may go wrong," he observed, "but good grub and a good tune before turning in smoothes over the rude excrescences, serving to make the toil of the woods a burden."

And what toil it was, six days a week in rain, snow, sleet or shine, "up and at em" at four in the morning. A half-hour later the cook blew his big tin horn for breakfast. By five o'clock the work in the woods had begun. Armed with double-bitted axes, choppers cut a nick in the big pine trees, and sawyers felled the forest giants with great cross cut saws. Swampers hacked off the tree limbs and sawyers cut the trunk into 16-foot-lengths. Skidders snaked the logs with teams of horses or oxen to the skids where loaders piled them onto sleighs. Teamsters hauled towering loads to the banking ground at the river's edge, where the following spring's rising current would start the season's cut

Shanty boys ate well in a good lumber camp. But the iron clad rule was "no talking at the table."

on its journey to the booming (sorting) grounds and awaiting sawmill.

At noon the huge, tin horn, known as the "Gabriel," signaled a quick meal and 15 minutes of rest. At dusk the weary men returned to camp for another hearty meal and an hour or so each evening for recreation before turning in at nine p.m. onto bunks containing blankets laid over straw.

Sunday brought the only day of rest, and, consequently, the boys "whooped it up" on Saturday night. The rough and randy loggers enjoyed equally rowdy entertainment. Before the fiddler tuned up for a "stag dance," with those designated the ladies tying a handkerchief around their arms, the men usually played games. One favorite Fitzmaurice described was known as "hot back" - during which:

> *One man bends over with his face hidden in a cap, and the rest all gather about him and strike, one at a time with all the possible force of the open hand upon the bosom of the victim's pants. If he can guess who struck the blow, the party thus caught has to bend over and take his place.*

An even worse experience awaited a newcomer or visitor to the camp who refused to sing a song or tell a story for the men's entertainment. The rule was he'd be "put up," that is thrown stomach down over one of the big log beams extending across the shanty and "while one holds his head and two others his feet, another pounds him on the distended bosom of his pants with a boot-jack."

Shanty boys had their own sense of right and wrong and their own brand of justice. Fitzmaurice recounted the time a "sky pilot", as itinerant preachers who evangelized among the loggers were called, visited a certain Michigan camp and proceeded to holler an after supper sermon while berating the men as to "how dirty they were, and how foul and polluted their habits and language was." He then requested the men to take up a little cash collection for him. When he left the room one of the "toughs"

A typical shanty boy bunk house of the late 19th century.

gathered the collection in a pill box as each shanty boy contributed a specimen of his personal "live stock." The next morning when the missionary was busy bent over shoveling down his breakfast, the "collector" emptied the box of "Michigan crumbs" down his exposed neck, and not a another word was said.

Despite his personal experiences as a Congregationalist minister, Fitzmaurice had little good to say about these itinerant preachers. "I have visited over 400 camps," he wrote, "and have yet to hear of or see one man who has expressed any benefit from the visit of the 'camp missionary.'"

As to the shanty boys themselves, Fitzmaurice summed up their character based on his many experiences:

> *Hard working, rough and ready, big hearted, generous, fraternal, impulsive, a hand for a friend, a foot for a foe, foolishly prodigal with hard earned wealth, happy under very questionable conditions for joy, sensitive to the sorrows of others more than his own, and faithful to his engagements when he is used with even moderate consideration and kindness.*

Incidentally, the morning after Fitzmaurice had been robbed of his jewelry, the Michigan shanty-boys returned every single piece with a hearty laugh and clap on the back for their new friend who had passed the test. ■

XVIII

WHEN IN PAIN - PLEASE PASS THE PAINE'S - HICCUP!

"The grave yawned wide" as Sarah S. Hoskins hovered "near death's door." It was in early 1891 that the prominent Paw Paw church woman began to go lame in her lower limbs. Within months she "could not walk across the house without the help of a cane." She developed "quite a cough," lost her appetite, and her "flesh wasted away." She and her friends thought, "I could live but a short time."

It was then that someone told her about Paine's Celery Compound, "the great nerve and brain strengthener and restorer." She limped down to G. W. Tyler's Drugstore and handed over a dollar for her first bottle emblazed with a huge head of celery, the crunchy vegetable long cherished as a folk medicine for nerve problems.

Before she had swallowed half a bottle's worth, a container that curiously resembled a fifth of whiskey, she "felt sure it was helping me." She improved rapidly and soon found herself walking without her cane down to Tyler's Drugstore for flask after flask of the wonderful elixir. When happily striding home from an evening social at the Paw Paw Free Baptist Church she met a friend who said, "It does beat all how well you are now! Do you really believe it was that celery compound medicine that did at all?" Sarah leaned forward and breathily whispered "I know it was, with the blessing of God attending it."

Wells, Richardson & Co. of Burlington, Vermont, the proprietors of the wonderful remedy, deeply appreciated Sarah's testimonial, so much so that they included it - along with an engraving of her likeness captioned in bold type "I want all the world to know of the medicine that saved my life" - in the company's special promotional pamphlet published in 1892.

What the Paw Paw church lady could not have known about the life saving elixir - because neither local, state or federal law required a statement of contents on the label - was that the Vermont proprietors had taken the precaution of augmenting celery's curative powers with the distilled essence of cocoa leaves, the source of cocaine. And to ensure that their bottles not burst during Michigan's cold winters they had incorporated 21% alcohol into the solution - purely as an antifreeze of course. Small wonder that the old lady felt "so well" after each dose.

Swigging the alcohol & drug laden Paine's brought Sarah Hoskins, a prominent Paw Paw church woman, back from "death's door."

Civil War General William Wells, his several brothers and A.E. Richardson founded a firm in 1872 to market wholesale drugs. Some time later they purchased the formula for a celery panacea from a Burlington widow, the mysterious Mrs. Paine. But by the early Twentieth Century the firm attributed its invention to a distinguished medical college professor, Edward E. Phelps, M.D. However the Paine name remained.

Thanks to a generous advertising budget and a slew of ebullient testimonials by users, the celery compound became a national best seller, rendering its producers very wealthy men. Sales remained strong for half a century, especially through the Prohibition era. Repeal of the Volstead Act in 1933 finally did it in. The firm had earlier diversified, adding profitable sidelines, "Diamond Dyes" for household coloring of cloth and "Lactated Food for Infants and Invalids," a "sure cure for cholera infantum," and these brought continued success after the demise of the celery compound.

But at the height of the celery medicine's profitability during the early 1890s a distressing number of competitors had begun horning in on the racket, most notably in Kalamazoo, Michigan.

Beginning in the 1850s, Dutch immigrants with large families essential in the labor intensive task of celery growing had developed the lush swampland surrounding Kalamazoo into choice muck plats. By the 1890s some 350 celery growers cultivated more than 4,000 acres, making Kalamazoo and environs the nation's largest single celery growing district.

Capitalizing on the "Celery City's" growing reputation, other entrepreneurs zeroed in on the patent medicine arena. The largest, the P.L. Abbey Co., bottled celery tonics at a 11,000 square-foot factory on Walbridge Street. The Hall Brothers invented Celerine Compound and Celery Compound which contained both celery and catnip. Others included the Kalamazoo Medicine Company's Celery Pepsin Bitters and the Quality Drug Stores' Kalamazoo Celery and Sarsaparilla Compound. All promised miraculous cures for wide ranging ailments.

Still others seized on celery's other folk medicine attribute - that it was a sexual stimulant. The Celery Medicine Co.

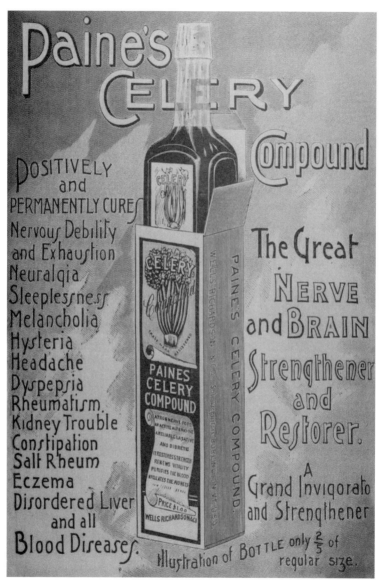

Paine's Celery Compound promised to be a virtual panacea.

Local entrepreneur Samuel J. Dunkley promoted his Celerytone elixir as a sexual stimulant.

promoted its Celery Tonic Bitters via trade cards depicting three sets of amorous couples aged seven, seventeen and seventy. Erstwhile local inventor Samuel J. Dunkley distributed post cards picturing storks delivering babies over celery fields, a less than subliminal advertisement for his Celerytone.

Back in Burlington, Vermont, the brothers Wells and Richardson were not about to let these usurpers gobble up the celery medicine market lying down. One of the last things he did, it seems, before old Gen. Wells died in April, 1892, was to level the company's promotional cannons at Michigan.

The company produced a 32-page pamphlet called *Our Album: Special Edition for Ohio and Michigan*. After an initial few pages of thumbnail sketches of "eminent men of Ohio and Michigan," including none other than Senator Francis B. Stockbridge of Kalamazoo, the publication commenced its real message - 31 half-page testimonials by satisfied Paine's Celery Compound users. Fully 27 of that number were Michiganders, revealing the actual thrust of the piece.

From Kalamazoo, Jefferson J. Wilder, a South Edwards Street jeweler, wrote that he had "been a great sufferer for many years from inflammatory rheumatism and nervous prostration." After spending "much money" on doctors, he "had given up hope." Following the quaffing of one bottle of Paine's, he became "a new man."

Testimonials from men such as Wilder were not the norm - women emerged as the real beneficiaries of the alcohol/narcotic cocktail - during an era that denied all but "bad ones" entrance through the swinging saloon doors that lined the streets of Kalamazoo and other Michigan communities. In the privacy of their homes, however, maidens, mothers and matrons could quaff medicine without even comprehending why Paine's made the day seem so much brighter.

From the Van Buren County hamlet of Glendale, Clara Butterfield wrote that "Death knocked at her door." First came a severe bout of the grippe (a contemporary term for influenza) followed by pneumonia which brought on heart trouble, "and my head would nearly go wild, it was so bad." A few bottles of Paine's later and, "I feel like a new woman."

In nearby Bangor, Mrs. M. E. Wright was "saved from awful agony." After five years of suffering from nerve and heart troubles, "with a terrible throbbing of my heart whenever trying to perform any kind of labor" and unable to sleep nights "on account of my nerves," a couple bottles of Paine's did the trick. Wright quoted her physician, Dr. J. Camp, as saying "he must confess that Paine's has performed a miracle in my case."

Another physician, 73-year-old Dr. D. W. Halstead from Adrian, doctored himself with the panacea. He was attacked by neuralgia in the kidneys, a paralyzed urethra and shaking palsy. "I thought that I should go crazy," he wrote. After taking Paine's he gained weight and felt "ten years younger." The doctor began prescribing it to ten of his patients with diverse diseases and, he assured, "they are all doing nicely." "May God bless you for sending out such a medicine," he wrote.

Of course, some stubborn cases required more of Paine's than others. It took ten bottles of the elixir to buoy up Nancy M. Prettyman of Berrien Springs. "It strengthened her nerves and did her a world of good," wrote her son, since his mother evidently felt so buoyant she, herself, could not pick up pen.

Similarly, Mrs. H. J. Fraker's husband wrote from Hastings that after despairing of treatment by several physicians 15 bottles of Paine's had rescued his wife "from slavery to sick headache."

No less than "thirteen of the best physicians" had told Mrs. M.J. Wise of Marshall that "there was no cure for me." Nine doses of Paine's later and "the pain left and I can go to bed and sleep all night." After downing only three bottles she noticed "I can sing quite a little." So grateful for her new state was she that "I would be willing to kiss the hem of the man's garment who made Paine's Celery Compound."

While consumers did not know the brown bottle's contents, the black-hearted Vermont bottlers did, and that knowledge did not prevent them from touting testimonials promoting Paine's as equally good for little children. In a Paine's advertisement headlined "Drooping with Disease," A. W. Fisher, a Bay City news reporter, testified that his three children Demott, Clarence and Florence, "did not seem to have any health whatever," But

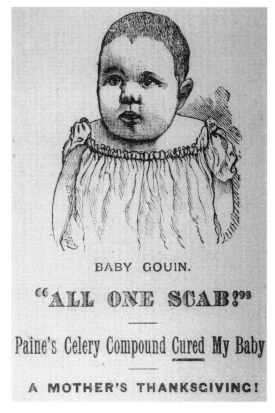

The Paine Company promoted its alcohol and narcotic mixture as ideal for this six month old sufferer.

following a "liberal use of the compound they now enjoy the best of health." "The compound," he added, "acts like magic in cases when children are run down, nervous and out of sorts."

More than one mother found the magical mixture ideal for quieting bawling babies, as well. Mrs. M.V. Gouin wrote from Detroit, "when my baby was six weeks old she was all one scab." Two weeks after spooning down Paine's the sores disappeared and "she is perfectly well." Ella Kress of Ypsilanti had not had a night's rest for eighteen months following the birth of her son. The tyke suffered from spasms and liver trouble and the family physician "never thought he could live." A week's worth of Paine's and "he commenced to gain" and is now "the picture of health," she wrote. So pleased was Ella that she and her mother began guzzling the stuff and also began to "sleep like children."

That a gulp or two of alcohol and cocaine would bring on sleep is small wonder. Peaceful slumber is a common thread through the testimonials. An old spinster from Paw Paw, Calista Hogmire, a name to be reckoned with, had suffered from various stomach and nerve complaints for 30 years before dosing herself with Paine's and soon finding, "I can sleep well nights." She added "it's a wonderful medicine and I have induced a great many to take it."

Whether Hogmire had been the one who turned on neighbor Sarah Hoskins to the panacea we can never know for sure. But what we do know is that the Rev. Mrs. Anna Barton signed a statement authenticating the truthfulness of Sarah's testimonial. The Rev. Barton was pastor of the Paw Paw Free Baptist Church, one of the few denominations that then allowed women to take the pulpit and one that had taken an early strong stand in favor of prohibition of alcohol.

Barton, herself, of a poetic turn of mind, had published a volume of verse, *For Friendship's Sake*, in Kalamazoo in 1882. A major section of the book includes her many poems promoting abstinence from alcohol. Typical of her effusions is this stanza from "Advice To Girls":

> *No lips shall ever press my own, that hold*
> *The cruel glass between their love and mine.*
> *No guide I'll trust across life's dangerous sea,*
> *Whose hand is weakened by his love of wine.*

Of course, celery flavored patent medicine was, evidently, another matter. ■

An 1892 newspaper advertisement celebrated the virtues of the alcohol laden medicine for children.

XIX

THE KID FROM KALAMAZOO & OTHER KNIGHTS OF THE ROAD

It was a sun-dappled summer's afternoon in the mid 1890s, the heyday of the hobo. At a certain hobo jungle secluded in the woods not far from the railroad tracks, one by one the tramps returned from a nearby town, each having begged a hot meal and with their pockets bulging with viands for the evening repast. William H. Davies, the Welsh poet and "Super-Tramp" who described in several autobiographies numerous forays into Michigan prior to falling off a train and losing a leg, had never known his friend, Detroit Fatty, to be in such a state of mind: "He was seen to bite his lip and to pass his hand over his forehead, and glare defiantly at his companions."

When Saginaw Slim tried to console him, "the poor fellow sat on a fallen tree and rocked his head between his hands." Bothered by their brother beggar's strange behavior, a trio of tramps demanded he tell them the problem. Whereupon Fatty pulled a small bar of soap from his pocket, threw it on the ground and in a broken voice explained the cause of his dejection:

> Boys, I am no longer fit for your company, for I have now become a common thief. When I was

leaving a certain house, I saw a small piece of soap on the window sill and, forgetting that I was a well-known beggar, and not a petty thief - I stole it. Can you keep the secret, boys? Let my guilt not be seen in the eyes of my fellow travelers when I enter into strange camps. In stealing this bar of soap I have proved myself an unsuccessful beggar and false to my profession, and I have certainly won no glory as a thief. I, who could beg half a ton of soap in a day, to be guilty of stealing this!

The disgraced pan-handler then kicked the soap into the woods, rushed from the camp and hopped a fast freight for parts unknown. After a lengthy discussion his companions concluded the thievery had been committed "in a temporary fit of insanity."

Davies's story demonstrated that some of the estimated half-million "men on the move," who rode the nation's rails during this era took a definite pride in their craft. But a well defined hierarchy existed among America's vagabonds, and all did not subscribe to such a high moral code as Detroit Fatty. Edmond Kelly, a professor at Columbia University and author of *The Elimination of the Tramp* (1908), offered these definitions of the general term vagrant: Tramp - one who dreams and wanders. Hobo - one who works sometimes and wanders. Bum - one who drinks and wanders.

By the end of the 20th century, tramps, hoboes, bums, the whole kit and caboodle, would be homogenized into the euphemisms, homeless or street person, and with the advent of the feminine version, bag lady.

But back in the golden age of trampdom the peripatetic brotherhood identified in its own colorful jargon each of the subspecies. Bindle stiffs carried a bundle containing all their worldly possessions - the stereotypical hobo of cartoons. Boomers were itinerant seasonal laborers. Dingbats and moochers were professional tramp beggars. A scenery bum was a young tramp traveling for the pleasure and excitement of it. Yeggs were dangerous professional criminals who moved among the railroad tramps and were not above murdering their fellow

A stereotypical tramp/bum as depicted on this cartoon postcard mailed to a man in Chesaning, Michigan, in 1907.

travelers. At the bottom were jungle buzzards who subsisted on food left in camps after the tramps moved on or actually begged off other hoboes.

A successful professional beggar soon learned who were the most likely to succumb to his plea for help. One turn-of-the-century scholarly tramp devised a ranking of the best "marks." He suggested beggars approach laborers or shabby looking men because "the less wealthy prefer to believe they belong to a class that gives rather than a class that receives." Prostitutes, he testified, were the most generous because they liked to atone for their sins with acts of generosity. Catholic sisters, too, were particularly good-natured toward the needy. Protestant clergymen, on the other hand, were to be avoided as "they will raise your hopes, waste your time, and send you along with nothing more than pompous commandments."

Josiah Strong's 1899 autobiography depicted typical "tomato-can tramps."

Joseph Cook, a clergyman who spent some time among tramps in the 1870s gathering material for a sermon he delivered in Boston against them, learned the meaning of the cabalistic symbols hoboes chalked on the gates of homes. A single circle meant the household was good for food and clothing. A circle with one line through it meant that a beggar could only get food. A circle with two lines meant beware, a vicious dog abided there, anathema to beggars.

Nuggets of lore about tramps, hoboes and the ilk abound throughout Michigan's literary heritage. Among the earliest recorded is a territorial law enacted in 1818 providing for stern punishment of "any idle vagrant." Tramps apprehended by a constable were to be tied to the whipping post near Detroit's market place on Woodward Avenue and lashed "not exceeding ten stripes." An alternative sentence provided for each to be auctioned off to the highest bidder as a slave for up to three months time. An 1821 article in the Detroit *Gazette* noted that the law "has had the effect of sending from the territory very many drunkards and vagabonds that thronged into it from Canada, Ohio and the state of New York." The punitive vagrancy law remained in effect for 20 years.

After the Civil War a pandemic of tramps rambled the countryside, begging or stealing, facilitated in their travels by the national networks of railroads that had been laid beginning in the 1830s. Grand Rapids pioneer and Civil War hero Charles Belknap remembered "the country including Western Michigan was infested with hundreds of wandering men who wandered the continent over, sleeping any place at all and living on back door lunches and the sympathies of the public." Many vagabonds were, in fact, disabled Union soldiers during an era when a government pension for total disability paid only $8 a month. Belknap noted that after the Michigan Soldiers Home for indigent veterans opened in Grand Rapids in 1886, the army of veteran tramps diminished.

Belknap recalled another set of factors that influenced tramps to seek their livelihood in areas other than southwest Michigan, the "three S's" - soap, soup and swatter - the first two supplied at workhouses to which judges sentenced tramps, and

Vigilante justice for tramps on the Michigan frontier sometimes included a "timber lesson."

Edwin A. Brown masqueraded as a tramp in 1911 to explore Detroit's homeless situation.

they often featured an actual rock pile to be pounded into road gravel. The swatter came in the form of beatings with clubs, sometimes administered by vigilante bands of locals. Belknap remembered a tramps' lodging house on lower Monroe Street where "for five cents a man could have two by six feet on the floor." Another nickel bought the use of a thin blanket for the night.

Elsewhere in Michigan Edwin A. Brown masqueraded as a tramp to gather information for his 1913 volume *"Broke" The Man Without the Dime*, an expose of the plight of urban homeless. During the bitterly cold winter of 1911-1912 he spent a week investigating Detroit. He found the mission established by wealthy philanthropist Tracy McGregor to be one of the best in the nation with the exception that early on a Sunday morning the scantily clad inmates were driven outside to shiver in the cold for two hours. Worse yet, at the Michigan Free Employment Bureau, where applicants stomped in with snow encrusted feet, he observed "two hundred crowded into a congested room - many of them with broken shoes and sockless feet standing in ice water for hours while they waited and hoped!"

Those without even a nickel or dime for a flop house or who found themselves in a rural environment when winter hit often chose to commit some petty crime and thus gain sanctuary in the local lock-up. In 1878 the Coldwater *Republican* reported that 50 tramps were being housed and fed at taxpayer's expense in the Branch County Jail.

After spending a season harvesting fruit in Berrien County, super-tramp Davies enjoyed a cozy winter in the local hoosegow though the machinations of a crooked sheriff who was only too happy to take in any and all tramps and then pocket most of the per diem the county allotted for each prisoner.

In his delightful memoir about growing up in Berrien County's Hartford, the heart of the fruit country, Kalamazoo historian Willis Dunbar described the hoboes and tramps who streamed into the town during harvest time. He termed them "for the most part the scum of the earth." They went house to house pretending to seek work, some claiming to be skilled at repairing lawn mowers, "but few of them wanted to get on the business end of one." Rather than arrest them for some minor infraction and lodge the vagrants in jail at village expense, the local marshal raided the jungle down near the railroad yards and chased them away.

Other southwestern Michigan communities adopted a seemingly ideal remedy to repel men who did not like to work - the stone pile. On January 12, 1901, the editor of the Grand Haven *Tribune* advised: "The tramp problem is a mounting concern for the county... Allegan has the rock pile in place and working. The supervisors are contemplating setting up an area for stones which could occupy their stay in the county jail. This might convince the genius hobo to stay clear of Grand Haven and Ottawa County."

By that date Kalamazoo already had a stone pile in place for vagrants to learn the value of blistered hands. In a well researched history of early Vicksburg, Mabel Hawkins related the story of a how a certain Deputy Clark solved the case of four tramps guilty of breaking seals to enter boxcars. In July 1897 they had been caught in the act by a conductor who doused them with a pail of water. Clark rounded up all the tramps in the vicinity, 58 in all, and sent along the four wet ones to Kalamazoo and 30 days working on the city's stone pile.

Other law enforcement officers were not so successful in dealing with tramps. In 1899, Night Policeman John Craig attempted to arrest a pair of tramps hiding in a boxcar on the Sturgis siding. Two shots rang out, killing the patrolman. Despite an intensive manhunt involving a posse of 100 men and a $500 reward, the murderers escaped apprehension.

The most infamous gang of yeggs, the "Lakeshore Push" (an underworld term for gang), operated mainly along the Michigan Southern and Lakeshore Railroad, which ran, in part, from Toledo across southern Michigan and hence to Chicago. Josiah Flynt, who described in several books his career both as a tramp and tramp detective in the 1880s and 90s, wrote in detail about the Lakeshore Push. Beginning in the 1870s through the turn-of-the-century, the gang robbed scores of merchandise cars, banks, post offices and homes, and fled with virtual impunity on the railroad. Many of the gang's members were tough Great Lakes sailors without work when the shipping season ended in the fall.

But for every yegg there were dozens of relatively honest "knights of the road" who embraced the hobo lifestyle for the freedom and adventure it offered. Some were even lovable characters, such as Harry Cooper, a.k.a. Railroad Jack, an intellectual hobo who is credited with inventing a hammock for riding safely strapped beneath the boxcars. Beginning in 1889 he rode the rail on 58 different railroad lines across the nation, logging a total of 130,000 miles. When not on his peregrinations

A "City Tramp" accosting his "mark."

Among the thrills and dangers of hobo life was a ride on a "truck" beneath the railroad car.

Harry, who possessed near total recall of the many history books he had absorbed, delivered well-received lectures atop a soapbox in the streets of Bay City, Detroit and other Michigan cities. He became a particular favorite among the students at the University of Michigan, who crowded around him during his orations and peppered him with historical questions which he never failed to answer correctly. Railroad Jack jumped his last train in 1933 and was found dead beside the tracks in Coldwater. His grave, marked with a handsome tombstone contributed by an admirer, lies in Ann Arbor's St. Thomas Catholic Church Cemetery.

The number of tramps traveling by train leveled off after World War I with the proliferation of automobiles and the emergence of an alternative free way to ride, "bumming" via the thumb.

The Great Depression, however, witnessed an increase in the number of vagabonds who rode the rails. With jobs nearly impossible to find, especially in hard-hit Michigan, many a young man and some girls, too, took to the road for adventure. Thomas Minehan's *Boy and Girl Tramps of America*, published in 1934, documented in a survey that only Pennsylvania contributed more young tramps than Michigan. Minehan included a number of pages concerning his interview of a young hobo with the moniker Kalamazoo Kid, a teenaged Casanova who boasted loudly of his under-age conquests.

By the Depression era, a considerable body of tramp poetry had been collected, and some of it featured the likes of "Big Mac from Mackinaw," "Con the Sneak from Battle Creek," and "Lonesome Lou from Kalamazoo." Evidently, there existed more than one hobo who adopted the nickname, Kalamazoo Kid. In 1937, Loren Phillips published his volume, *Songs of the Cinder Trail*, which included a poetic saga of "The Kid from Kalamazoo," who, not unlike Detroit Fatty, cherished a certain pride in his craft. After begging a dime from a stranger the Kid replied:

> "Bo, I aint no woikin stiff, I'll have ye understand!"

Said he: "I am a gentleman, cut out fer higher things
Than woikin' fer me board an' keep like common underlings;
These hands o' mine aint done no woik fer lousy profiteers;
I've been a knight o' th' roarin' road fer nigh on thirty years!
They call me th' Kid from Kalamazoo, an 'ever bo y' meet
'Il tell ye I have got a style that none uv em c'n beat;
T' hit a backdoor fer a handout, I wuz never knowed,
Fer I aint jest a common bum, - I'm a knight o' th' roarin' road!" ■

A youthful hobo hops a train.

XX

Michigan's Better Angel

It had not been easy growing up "different" in Barton, Michigan, during the early years of the twentieth century. For as long as he could remember, adolescent Kurt Gray had not been interested in the things other boys his age liked. Where they could be hard and cruel, he was soft and kind-hearted and, of course, suffered near constant teasing at school because of that and his lily white skin. Inept at sports, after the humiliation of attempting to play baseball or football, "more than likely, he headed for the big chair in the front window with a storybook."

Kurt's father, editor of the local newspaper, showered him with the best brands of athletic equipment. They went unused or were given to neighboring boys. Puzzled and hurt, the elder Gray wondered, but never articulated, "Why should his son be so different? Why, he was like a girl?"

His mother, who doted on her only child, attempted to console him in his fear of ridicule by schoolmates and to instill a sense of superiority. "Why do you want to be like other boys, Kurt?" she would ask. "Everybody who amounts to anything is different." And gradually, with her backing, he began to acquire a sense of pride in his difference, but still, except for his treasured books and a few other pleasures, he mostly suffered a lonely childhood.

Among those other pleasures was an near innate love of theatre. He constructed miniature stage sets with cutout dolls as actors. He wrote and directed elaborate plays staged in the loft of a nearby carriage house, acted out by a few younger children of the neighborhood, who, unlike his peers, did not constantly ridicule him.

Life got easier for the different boy in high school. He found himself welcomed into a clique of about a dozen sons and daughters of middle class and professional people in the little town couched within the sinuous coils of the Kalamazoo river. The tough kids who had tormented him in grade school were mostly gone. Kurt explained why:

Forman Brown posed for a publicity photograph, ca. 1928.

> *The factories were the cause of that. Their doors were always open for young muscles, strong bodies, nimble fingers; and the temptation of twelve dollars each week and the attendant independence that such a salary and such a life seemed to involve was a strong one. So as soon as they were sixteen many of them bought overalls and drill aprons and dinner pails and become slaves of the whistle as they had been slaves of the bell. Often when Kurt had occasion to go on the far side of the river, where the paper mills and the shoe factory and the cabinet workers were, he would see older boys he had avoided in school - stripped to the waist, their bodies shining with sweat, moving through the weird scene of billowing steam and the acrid smell of disinfectant, pushing trucks of paper or snatching a breath of air at one of the open windows. It was a hot unhealthy place, the paper mill. Beaters were the worst, reeking with steam and bleach, but it was all abnormally humid and odorous. In the sorting rooms, where fingers flew through bags of refuse and rags, or through long grimy windows at the clicking stitching machines of the shoe factory, he would see girls who were not so much older than he.*

Kurt graduated in 1918, as class valedictorian, and entered the University of Michigan. His mother had arranged for him to room with a woman who had been the wife of a minister in Barton before moving with her son and daughter to Ann Arbor. Kurt got along well with the boy, Derry who was his own age and of similar interests, and by the spring 1919 he had his first homosexual liaison with him.

Kurt Gray is the hero of a novel, *Better Angel*, pseudonymously written by Richard Meeker, whose real identity long remained a mystery. Published in New York in 1933, it became an underground classic, considered "the first novel published in America to show male homosexuality in a positive lights - it even provided its gay hero with an apparently happy ending." Retitled *Torment* and reprinted as a tawdry paperback in the 1950, *Better Angel* reappeared in a scholarly edition published in Boston in 1987. Not long afterwards, Forman Brown finally outed himself as the author. He wrote an epilogue for a 1995 edition of the novel in which he admitted that, "like so many first novels, mine was largely autobiographical." He revealed the names of the real life people portrayed as characters (including one bisexual he had a brief fling with who later married Gypsy Rose Lee) and that Barton was, in fact, Otsego, Michigan.

Born January 8, 1901, the first child born in the twentieth century in Otsego, he was the son of George R. and Pet Brown. The elder Brown published the Otsego *Union* from 1897 to 1929. The details of Forman Brown's life while growing up at their home at 303 Orleans Street in Otsego are well documented in *Better Angel*. He also wrote another autobiographical work, *Punch's Progress*, under his real name. Published in 1936, it relates the story of the traveling puppet troupe he and fellow students Harry Burnett and Richard Brandon (real life characters in *Better Angel*, as well,) launched while at the University of Michigan. During summer recesses the threesome toured resorts along Lake Michigan; Saugatuck, Macatawa, Muskegon, Manistee, Petoskey, Cheboygan and Mackinac Island, setting up a portable stage and delighting growing audiences with their puppetry.

Following graduation from the University of Michigan in 1922, Brown spent a brief stint as an instructor at North Carolina State College, toured Europe and then rejoined the love of his life, in New Haven, Connecticut, where Burnett had formed the Yale Puppeteers. By the late 1920s, the Yale Puppeteers had opened a theatre on Oliver Street in Los Angeles, and they soon enjoyed an enthusiastic following which included movie stars Greta Garbo, Marie Dressler and Douglas Fairbanks.

In the meantime Brown had written a book of poetry, *Walls*, printed by his father's press in Otsego in 1925. His poetry won praise by Robert Frost, Frank Harris and other literati. In 1929, a

Otsego's rutted East Allegan St., ca. 1908.

Chicago publisher printed his second poetry collection, *Spider Kin*. Brown's alma mater included three of his poems in *New Michigan Verse*, published in Ann Arbor in 1940.

The following year Brown and the other Yale Puppeteers founded the Turnabout Theatre in Hollywood to stage adult programming. Unique in that it contained two stages, one on either end of the auditorium, the theatre featured swivel seats so that when the puppet show ended the audience would reverse direction to view the "Turnabout Revue." Brown wrote all the songs and sketches featured, including more than fifty numbers for Elsa Lanchester, who joined the troupe on a permanent basis.

The real-life characters from Brown's 1933 novel, Better Angel, *posed about the time it was published.*

The theatre become a favorite with famous Hollywood stars, and one wall was devoted to autographs of those who had attended. The Turnabout Theatre thrived until 1956.

In the 1990s a documentary film about the Turnabout Theatre and the many popular songs and skits Brown wrote brought renewed interest in his work. Bette Midler sang one of Brown's most requested piece's, "Mrs. Pettibone," at an AIDS benefit in Los Angeles.

Following her husband's death in 1929, Brown's beloved mother spent the last 20 years of her life living with her son in Los Angeles. In 1957, Richard Meyer had reviewed *Torment* in the pioneering gay journal, *Mattachine Review*, and prophesized, "I wouldn't bet that [the hero and his lover] lived happily ever after." He was wrong. The man considered "one of the world leaders in puppet theatre in his day," died two days after his 95th birthday in 1996.

The demise of this nationally famous celebrity who had spent his formative years in Otsego went unheralded by any Allegan County newspaper. ■

The frontispiece from Brown's 1929 collection of poetry, Spider Kin.

XXI

THE ROAMER, "AMERICA'S SMARTEST CAR"

America's original motion picture female mega-star, Mary Pickford, could afford any car she wanted. So she ordered a Roamer; a custom-built, sleek, cream-colored speedster built in Kalamazoo and complete with a huge turquoise set into the horn button. Seated behind the wheel of the jaunty classic powered by a muscular Deusenberg engine, "America's Sweetheart" gaily waved to Hollywood admirers.

Other matinee idols, including Buster Keaton and Wallace Beery, chose flashy Roamers as did Arabian sheiks, Turkish sultans, Indian rajahs, British peers, German counts and moneyed manufacturing moguls across America. Former President William Howard Taft squeezed his portly frame into the back seat of a Roamer during his 1921 visit to Kalamazoo and really gave the springs a test.

The madcap Roaring Twenties marked a brief but glorious era in Kalamazoo's industrial annals when hundreds of skilled mechanics assembled "America's smartest car."

The Roamer was the brainchild of Midwestern entrepreneur Albert C. Barley, who launched his business career as a merchant in Marion, Indiana. In 1902, he dabbled in selling some of the new-fangled horseless carriages that had caught the nation's fancy. Three years later he became a director of the Rutenber Motor Co., a pioneer manufacturer of automobile gas engines.

Via those endeavors and through ownership of a variety of automobiles, he caught the mechanical fever, and in 1912, decided to try his hand at manufacturing his own brand of motorcar. He bought out the Streator Motor Car Co. of Streator, Illinois., which had been producing the Halladay since 1907. The newly renamed Barley Manufacturing Co. continued to build improved versions of the Halladay until 1916, ultimately adopting 50-horsepower Rutenber engines in three chassis sizes.

Not satisfied with the Halladay's design, Barley conceived the ideas behind the Roamer, that of "making a car high-grade mechanically, distinctive in design, finished and trimmed to meet the requirements of each individual purchaser, and at a price that would be within reach of men of average means." Securing top-notch engineering talent, by 1914 Barley had developed the prototype Roamer. It was a hybrid machine assembled from the finest available engine, transmission, clutch, brakes, springs and frame.

A rakish 1922 Roamer powered by a Deusenberg engine.

Barley designed a special body style which yielded a roomy interior fitted with cushiony leather-covered seats. Despite Barley's goal to make the vehicle affordable for the average buyer, the Roamer evolved into a relatively expensive luxury car modeled after the Rolls-Royce. It boasted a big, silvery radiator frame, a long, sloping hood and plenty of nickel-plated hardware and trim.

Originally conceived to compete in the export market, sample Roamers displayed in Paris and London drew favorable reviews. But when the outbreak of World War I halted sales overseas, Barley shifted to the domestic arena and established an agency in New York City.

In 1916, the Barley Motor Car Co. was incorporated in New York with a capital of $200,000 in stock. By 1918 full page advertisements in up-scale New York theatre bills pitched the automobile to a snooty client:

> *You can ransack the country and not find another American-made car like the Roamer. The Roamer possesses a desirable tone of aloofness - of utter indifference from any other American motor car - which makes ownership peculiarly pleasant.*

But as the sporty Roamer began to catch the fancy of well-to-do Americans, Barley found his manufacturing facilities in Streator inadequate.

In the meantime, Kalamazoo entrepreneurs had been diligently attempting to secure for their hometown a share in the automotive bonanza that would ultimately produce some 2,500 different makes of cars.

In 1902, two sets of brothers, Frank and Charles Fuller and Maurice and Charles Blood, formed the Michigan Automobile Co. to manufacture a little golf cart-like contraption. Two years later, the Blood brothers left the firm to establish their own factory. The Blood evolved into a much heavier vehicle which sold for $1,500.

In 1920, Albert Barley paid to insert this full page advertisement in a history of Kalamazoo County's role in WWI.

In 1903, Frank Burtt and Warren B. Cannon teamed up to produce the Cannon Flyer. Unfortunately, in the highly competitive automotive industry none of those early Kalamazoo attempts survived more than a few years.

For decades Kalamazoo had enjoyed a booming business in horse-drawn carriages, and as the automobile brought hard times to that industry, some firms like the massive Michigan Buggy Co. attempted to switch over to production of horseless carriages. By 1913 a $350,000 advertising campaign promoted the "Mighty Michigan" in full page *Saturday Evening Post* advertisements. But by the year's end the big factory on Reed and Factory streets closed its doors, and 553 employees were without jobs.

Determined that Kalamazoo would not suffer industrial atrophy, the Chamber of Commerce launched a campaign to lure a tenant into the huge empty factory. Four years later that effort paid off when the Kalamazoo *Gazette* announced that Barley would relocate his operations to the buggy plant and begin full scale production of the Roamer. The chamber quickly raised the $5,000 moving expense money it had pledged, and a few weeks later a long train loaded with Barley's machinery chugged into the city.

By 1919 approximately 125 employees were assembling 1,500 cars annually. The following year the workforce had increased to 350. The company announced a goal of selling 5,000 Roamers that year.

In an age when Henry Ford and other high volume manufacturers were preaching the gospel of mass-production, assembly-line techniques, Barley capitalized on the appeal of custom-made quality craftsmanship. Consumers could chose powerful Deusenberg or Continental engines, fancy wire wheels, avant-garde accessories such as electric dashboard clocks and window wipers and, by 1925, nine body styles ranging from the touring car at $2,495 to the special sedan at $3,785.

During an era when "get out and get under" still applied to motoring, most models came with three spare tires, one mounted on each side and one in the rear. And contrary to the standard

This model F-28 Roamer set a world's record of 105.2 mph at Daytona Beach in 1921. (Courtesy Western Michigan University Archives.)

black paint other manufacturers specified, Roamer buyers could order the vehicle in robin egg blue, bright red or any other color scheme they desired to make their vehicle "stand out." In 1917, a Los Angeles mogul ordered his Roamer painted bright orange striped in white. Three Roamers, one painted red, one white and one blue, led several Kalamazoo parades in the early 1920s.

Beginning in 1919, Barley began competing for publicity on the racing circuit. The company hired Roscoe Sarles, famed driver Louis Chevrolet's riding mechanic, to race Deusenberg-powered Roamers. Sarles broke a course record to win a 100-mile race at the Ascot Speedway in Los Angeles on Jan. 26, 1919. In March he broke another record on the same track to finish first in a 150-mile race.

Memorial Day of 1919 found two Roamers entered in the Indianapolis 500. The one driven by Kurt Hitke, plant superintendent in Kalamazoo, dropped out after 140 miles when a bearing burned out. The other Roamer piloted by Louis Le Cage and Bob Bandini made it to the 96th lap when the race car struck the concrete wall and burst into flames. Both drivers died in the crash. Not long after that tragedy Barley withdrew company support from the racing circuit.

But the following year came another racing venture, this time against the stopwatch, that would make Kalamazoo the talk of the industry. At Daytona Beach, Florida, on the morning of April 22, 1921, the Kalamazoo plant's aptly-named chief engineer, Leland F. Goodspeed, climbed into a strictly stock Roamer speedster equipped with the standard 70-horsepower, four-cylinder Deusenberg engine. With a roar of its exhaust, the car sped across the sand to establish a one mile straightaway record of 105.1 mph as well as four other world records.

The Barley Motor Car Co. appeared to be a winner in every way during the early 1920s. In 1922, the company introduced a cheaper version called the Barley and a Pennant line of taxicabs. Then in 1923 Barley consolidated his interests in the automobile company and the Kalamazoo Realty Company he had also invested in.

That strange combination of assets seemed to indicate that all was not well with the company's bottom line. The following

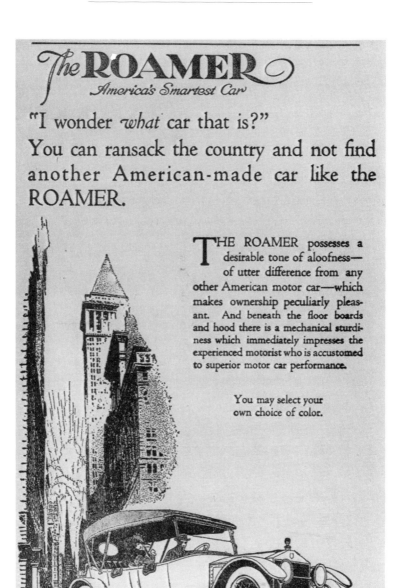

This roamer advertisement made a pitch to up-scale New York theatre patrons.

January, Barley stepped down as president and the company was reorganized with Kalamazoo Looseleaf Binder Co. CEO George P. Wigginton at its helm. Within a year, the Roamer Motor Car Co. of Canada purchased the Kalamazoo assets. Roamer production continued at a reduced pace in the Reed Street factory with California the principal market.

Then, in August 1927, the company paraded through Kalamazoo streets the prototype of its new Roamer sports tourer. The sleek model could cruise at 90 mph and carried a price tag of $14,500. But in an era when new Model T Fords retailed at less than $300, the Roamer was moving in the wrong direction. There were simply not enough customers willing to pay that kind of money for an automobile, regardless of its quality.

In 1928 the Roamer Motor Car Co. assets were taken over by a Delaware corporation. The company limped along in Kalamazoo, merchandising replacement parts for a few more years, then disappeared forever from the city's industrial roster, leaving only cherished memories of "America's Smartest Car." ■

XXII

A BELATED REBUTTAL ON RUSSIA

Gerald O. Dykstra, a 21-year-old Allegan man, stood on a makeshift platform while scanning the sea of 3,000 upturned faces assembled in his honor at the city of Ticharetzkaya, deep in the Russian steppes. It was a summer's evening in 1927.

The fete began with a brass band marching at the head of 300 Caucasian soldiers who passed in review. Then came speeches of welcome and a forum discussion with questions and answers, at the conclusion of which the crowd burst into a joyful rendition of the "Internationale."

> *Arise ye members of starvation!*
> *Arise, ye wretched of the earth!*
> *For justice thunders condemnation.*
> *A better world's in birth ...*

Dykstra remembered that occasion as the highlight of his six-week-long, 4,000-mile tour of the Soviet Union. The following year he published in Allegan a 196-page volume entitled, *A Belated Rebuttal On Russia*, an eloquent plea, based on his experiences, for American recognition of the Soviet government.

Born in Allegan in 1906 to Baker Furniture Co. craftsman Garrit Dykstra and his wife, Martha, young Dykstra had attended

Gerald O. Dyksta posed in typical Russian garb in 1927.

the old Dawson Elementary School which stood at the present site of the Allegan Fire Department. Following graduation from Allegan High School he enrolled in Albion College. Dykstra joined the Albion College debate squad in 1925 and the issue being discussed — whether America should recognize the Soviet government-spurred in him a passionate interest in everything Russian.

He transferred to the University of Michigan the following year and after graduation in 1927 was fortunate enough to secure permission to visit the Soviet Union through the Russian Society for Cultural Relations with Foreign Countries. Traveling with 14 other American professors and students, Dykstra sailed from New York to Glasgow, Scotland, then spent a few days touring parts of Europe before embarking on a German ship for the 700-mile voyage across the Baltic Sea to Leningrad.

Despite the fact that soldiers of the Polar Bear Division, largely recruited from Michigan, had fought in support of the Russian White Army after World War I had officially ended and otherwise meddled in the internal affairs of the new Soviet Republic, the Russian government and people welcomed Dykstra and his tour group with open arms.

Dykstra was allowed to go where he wanted, talk to anyone, take pictures and, in general, inspect the workings of the Communist regime to his heart's content. He visited Moscow and other major Russian cities, toured museums, factories and cathedrals, most of which had been converted to other uses, enjoyed a leisurely boat trip down the Volga River to Stalingrad, journeyed by train across the interior of the vast nation and crossed the Caucasus Mountains by automobile.

Contrary to expectations, he found a happy people, imbued with patriotic zeal over their novel experiment in government. Food was abundant as were many consumer items. True, even then customers had to wait in long queues for access to restaurants, stores, museums, and the like, but that, he learned, had also been the Russian way under the czars.

Dykstra enjoyed traditional Russian culinary treats. He sampled borsch, a soup made from beets and cabbage, and shchee, a type of vegetable soup, smoked fish and marvelous

Dykstra described strong, black, rye-bread, baked in giant loaves and sold in Leningrad markets.

black rye bread baked in loaves the size of a wash tub. He sipped strong tea brewed in charcoal samovars, thick, sweet Turkish Java, excellent local wines and, of course, the national drink, vodka.

In Moscow, Dykstra toured Nikolai Lenin's mausoleum where three years after his death and for many ensuing decades, the architect of the Russian Revolution remained laid out in state. Shortly thereafter he met an old man who had personally known Lenin. Dykstra asked him, "In the states it is said that you over here are making a god of Lenin. Is that true?" The old Russian responded: "No, Lenin is not a god to us, he is more than a god. For God only judges, but Lenin both judged and did."

Dykstra returned to Allegan satisfied that not only should America recognize the Communist government but that for anyone with capital and industrial ability his advice was "Go to Russia!" Finally, in 1933, the U.S. government granted formal recognition to the Soviet Union. The Russia that Dykstra experienced, however, would not last.

Lenin's "New Economic Policy" (NEP), which allowed internal freedom of trade, small individually operated farms, and private commercial establishments, in essence, an amalgam of socialism and capitalism, would end with the rise of Stalin. In 1928, Joseph Stalin abolished the NEP in favor of drastic "five-year plans" geared toward development of heavy industry at the expense of consumer goods, state operated collective farms and purges of all who stood in his way. The halcyon era viewed by Dykstra soon turned to decades of misery for the Russian people.

Following publication of his book in Allegan, Dykstra became a professor of business law at the University of Michigan. Blake "Bink" Perrigo of Allegan studied under Dykstra while he attended the U-M in the early 1960s. He remembered him as one of the most popular professors on campus, delivering lectures so entertaining that some students brought their dates to class.

Dykstra died in 1970, his wife, Lillian, followed in 1981, and now they lie side by side in the family plot in Allegan's Oakwood Cemetery. ■

Dykstra thought pretty Russian girls "really nice." Here he is seen with his "first Russian date."

XXIII

CASS COUNTY'S CRUSADING CORRESPONDENT

Webb Miller handed his cigarette case to the "little brown man" and asked him to pencil his signature within. Mahatma Gandhi eyed it closely, chuckled, and replied: "Why, this is a cigarette case, isn't it? You know what I think about the use of tobacco. I would not want my name covered with tobacco. If you will promise never to put cigarettes in it, I will sign it for you."

Miller agreed and converted it to a card case. Alongside Gandhi's signature were those of Georges Clemenceau, David Lloyd George, Gen. John Pershing, Adolph Hitler, Benito Mussolini and other world figures, good and evil, who Miller met during his career as one of America's most illustrious foreign correspondents of the era between the world wars.

Born in 1892, at a tenant farm near the Cass County hamlet of Pokagon, about five miles southwest of Dowagiac, Miller spent his youth assisting his father, Jacob, and mother, Charlotte, in the backbreaking and never ending cycle of eking a living from the various farms the family rented. Despite growing up in a bookless home, early on Miller fell in love with reading, borrowing classics from neighbors. Henry Thoreau's *Walden* proved a great influence on the development of his personal philosophy and throughout his world travels he carried a copy with him. In 1903 Dowagiac received $12,000 from Andrew Carnegie to build the city's first public library. When it opened, Miller walked ten miles round trip, sometimes through snow covered roads, to borrow the wonderful volumes that lined the library shelves.

A sensitive youth, Miller grew nauseous at the idea of consuming the flesh of animals. He became the only member of the family of seven who practiced strict vegetarianism. Later in life he abandoned the practice because of the attention his meat abstinence attracted.

Following graduation from Dowagiac High School, to which he had walked ten miles roundtrip many school days, Miller secured a summer position as pilot on a 90-foot passenger steamboat which plied Diamond Lake, a popular resort near Cassopolis. One dark and rainy night he crashed the vessel through a long pier that extended into the lake, with no injury to the passengers, but he nearly lost his job.

Webb Miller in 1936, when his biography I Found No Peace, *was published.*

The Dowagiac of Webb Miller's youth.

Miller's love of reading and writing ability (although writing was always hard for him, "I have to pull out each sentence by the roots," he once wrote) inspired him to become a newspaper man. In the autumn of 1911 he applied for a reporter's job at the South Bend *Tribune*, but was turned down. Instead he secured a position teaching in the Walnut Grove one-room school five miles south of Dowagiac. He taught all subjects to 12 pupils in grades one through eight at a salary of $40 a month.

The following summer Miller met Charles Fitzmorris, former editor of the Chicago *American*, who offered to try to get him a job in Chicago that fall. He boarded a boat in Benton Harbor and arrived in Chicago in 1912 with a pair of new suits and his life savings of $150. Several months later Fitzmorris got him a position as a cub reporter on the paper at a salary of $12 a week. The city editor made him a "leg man" who took assignments, gathered information and telephoned it to re-writers in the office. His beat embraced the seamy side of Chicago, the underworld of petty thieves, prostitutes, gangsters and murderers.

In 1914, he covered the hanging execution of a murderer, an experience that left the sensitive Michigan farm boy "unnerved and bewildered, with a shaky sensation at the pit of my stomach." He pleaded with his editor to assign him to another line of duty. The editor refused, explaining: "That's the reason you are a good reporter on such things. The more you hate it, the better job you do."

The biggest story he covered in Chicago was the *Eastland* disaster on July 24, 1915. Overloaded with 2,500 excursionists, mostly women and children, the St. Joseph, Michigan-based steamer rolled over on its side in 21-feet of water while docked in the Chicago River. Hundreds clawed for their lives in the swift current, and hundreds more were trapped within the vessel as the water rose. For 20 hours Miller sat on the side of the ship "writing brief descriptions of the limp, discolored bodies of men, women and children as they were hauled out of the interior through a hole cut through the steel hull." The final death toll of

The Eastland on its side in 1915, when 835 passengers perished.

835 made the *Eastland* tragedy the worst marine disaster in the history of the Great Lakes.

During his four year stint in Chicago, Miller embarked on a deliberate campaign of self improvement. He grew a moustache to make himself look older, changed his given name Webster to Webb for a better by-line and read his way through the 40-volume set of *Harvard Classics* he bought on the installment plan. Reading those world classics gave him an interest in other countries and he determined to become a foreign correspondent.

By 1916, he had had enough of the rough and tumble Chicago beat. He resigned and set out as a freelance writer to cover the punitive expedition under command of Gen. John Pershing in pursuit of the Mexican outlaw Pancho Villa. His success in covering that American military foray into Mexico became the first of a series of journeys which by the time he wrote his biography in 1936 would bring him to 41 countries on five continents.

In February, 1917, President Woodrow Wilson gave up on capturing Villa and the troops were withdrawn from Mexico. Miller went to work for the United Press (U.P.) syndicate. When Wilson signed the declaration of war against Germany on April 5, 1917, Miller learned from a reliable source in the War Department the true estimate of what the U.S. entry into the war would entail in men, money and munitions, information which was being kept from the American public at that time. Miller's UP story based on those facts seemed so absurd that most newspapers editors ignored it. Miller knew of only one editor in America who grasped the importance of the scoop. Rollo Britten, editor of the Manistee, Michigan, *News-Advocate*, ran the story under a huge black front page headline. But by the war's end in November, 1918, America had indeed learned the hard truth about World War I's impact.

The eighteen months Miller spent in Europe covering the war, often in front line positions, had a tremendous impact on his personality, making him "harder, more cynical, and had destroyed many illusions." But the "cataclysmic horror" of the war did not sink home until he toured the great European battlefields; Verdun, Meuse-Argonne, Chateau-Thierry, Belleau Woods, etc. in 1926. Miller described his bitter epiphany in his autobiography:

> *During the war I had been deluded, along with millions of others, by ignorance and propaganda, into believing that it really meant something, that it was a crusade to crush militarism, smash autocracy, and end war forever. But after eight years had passed militarism was obviously stronger than ever, greater more powerful autocracies were rising on all sides. The World War had succeeded only in breeding new wars. Eight and one-half million men had died in vain, tens of millions had suffered unutterable horrors, and hundreds of millions had undergone grief, deprivation, and unhappiness. And all this had happened under a stupendous delusion.*

From 1920-1925 Miller served as chief of the UP Paris bureau, then assistant European news manager in London for five years. In 1930 he became general European news manager responsible for UP coverage of the events that led to World War II. He personally reported some of the major economic and disarmament conferences, the Italian invasion of Ethiopia in 1935, the Spanish Civil War and the Munich Conference. Miller told a colleague that Neville Chamberlain's interpretation of the Munich Agreement as "peace in our time," was "simply absurd."

In May 1930, Miller had been dispatched to India to cover Gandhi's salt march to the sea, an episode in his decades long *Satyagraha* campaigns of civil disobedience to gain freedom for his people from the British. The march was a protest against the Salt Acts which made it illegal to possess any salt not heavily taxed by the government. Miller witnessed and reported on the brutal beating of hundreds of non-violent salt marchers at Dharasana, 150 miles north of Bombay. While in India Miller was unable to interview Gandhi because he had been arrested during his salt march.

Gandhi at the London Conference in 1931.

But the following year, when Gandhi attended a Round Table Conference in London, Miller had several long conversations with the "shriveled, little brown man" clad in his usual hand spun cotton *dhoti*. Miller recorded Gandhi description of his ascetic life style.

> *I rise at four a.m., pray for twenty minutes, write letters about an hour, take about half an hour's walk, and then, breakfast at six o'clock on goat-milk curds, dates, and raisins. Since the civil-disobedience campaign started I card, spin and sew cotton between six and nine. I made a vow to spin at least two hundreds yards of cotton every day. I want to influence our people to spin their own cloth and make themselves independent of importation from England. The largest single item of British importation into India is cotton cloth.*
>
> *At noon I lunch on bread, goat-milk curds, boiled vegetables, raw tomatoes, and almond paste, take a nap, and spend the afternoon in reading, meditation and receiving visits. I do not eat at night. Before my bedtime at nine-thirty I write in my diary. Until recently I always slept on the floor, but now I am old (he was then sixty-three) I sleep on an iron bed. Every Monday I have a day of silence; I speak to no person, no matter how urgent the matter may seem.*

During another lengthy conversation in Gandhi's hotel room, Miller was pleased to discover that they shared an appreciation of Thoreau's writings. Gandhi told him he read *Walden* in 1906 and it greatly influenced him. He admitted that Thoreau's classic essay "Civil Disobedience" proved of particular importance in the development of his own *Satyagraha* philosophy. He also appreciated that Thoreau had gone to jail for his beliefs, something that Gandhi was also subjected to many times.

In 1947, came the independence for India that Gandhi had fought so long and hard for. He was greatly saddened, however, by the simultaneous creation of Pakistan and the subsequent bloodshed between his own Hindus and Muslims. On January 30, 1948, a Hindu fanatic who opposed Gandhi's campaign of tolerance for all creeds, assassinated the saintly leader.

Eight years earlier, Miller had returned to London after covering the fighting on the Finnish front in order to report on the British cabinet crisis following the Nazi invasion of Norway. En route to his suburban home late one blackout night, he somehow stepped off a moving train and plunged to his death. His grave lies near his birthplace in Pokagon.■

Gandhi concentrating on his work, ca. 1932.

XXIV

OLD BONES & CANINE CUISINE

A canine chorus, yips, yaps, barks and howls, rose from the village below when Earl Richardson fired up his big backhoe. In quest of gravel, the snaggle-toothed bucket bit deep into the hilltop overlooking the ancient settlement of St. Ignace. Instead, bones dripped from its great metallic jaw - human skeletal remains.

It was early spring, 1958, and when news of the discovery reached University of Michigan archeologist Emerson F. Greenman he motored up from Ann Arbor, whizzing across the big bridge linking the Straits that had just been completed the year before. Greenman identified 52 native American skeletons buried in a communal grave in conjunction with a variety of artifacts including a stone tobacco pipe, a carved turtle shell effigy, brass bangles and numerous glass and copper beads. He estimated the date of the burial to be no less than three centuries before.

The archeologist concluded that the St. Ignace find marked the site of a "feast of the dead," a custom practiced by various Great Lakes cultures. As recorded by early Jesuit missionaries and Nineteenth Century fur traders such as Gurdon Hubbard, every ten years or so tribesmen would disinter from temporary graves the bones of those who had died since the previous feast. To female relatives fell the task of lovingly stripping from the cadavers any remaining flesh, then to clatter the bones into birchbark mococks and transport the bundles to a sacred site for mass reburial along with objects thought to be of value in the afterlife. The several-day-long ceremony featured grieving rituals, feasting, dancing, athletic events and orations by chiefs and family members of the decreased. Hubbard's account of the ceremony held at the mouth of the Grand River in 1819 included a description of an ancillary stabbing execution of a murderer by the victim's family.

Greenman secured the archeological evidence, believing the remains most likely to be from the Ottawa tribe, known to have had a village near the site in the late 1600s. Reports of another set of bones partially unearthed about 15-feet from the mass grave brought the archeologist back to St. Ignace in early May. This time the osseous remains proved to be those of a pair of dogs.

They had been buried on top of each other about 24 inches down. Forensic examinations revealed them to be large young canines. The skeleton of the lower one remained articulated, lacking only the bones of the feet. The upper skeleton was in a dismembered condition with the skull and some other bones missing. It became evident to Greenman that the dogs had played an important role in the feast of the dead ceremony - at least one, it appeared, had been on the menu of the feast.

The only North American animal to have been completely domesticated during pre-Columbian times, canines were an integral part of most aboriginal American cultures. A distinct breed that may well survive in the bloodlines of the scrawny, reddish-yellow, short coated, sharp-eared and whip-tailed mutts known as the "Carolina dog," Indian dogs assisted with the hunt, guarded crops and villages against predators, warmed the bed in winter and, like their ancestors since time immemorial, served as devoted and faithful companions. They also earned their keep as beasts of burden, carrying packs on their backs, pulling travois and in winter hitched to sleds as teams. When Great Plains Indians first saw Spanish dray horses they called them "big dogs." Utility, however, did not prevent more than one beloved pooch from finding its way into the stew pot.

Joseph Lafitau's 1724 history of the Indians included a fanciful depiction of the "Feast of the Dead."

Flavius Littlejohn's collection of Indian tales published in Allegan in 1875 pictured a domestic scene, including dogs, near Three Rivers.

Written accounts by numerous witnesses document the consumption of dogs, and white dogs, it seems, were particularly revered for their spiritual and or gustatory qualities. French fur trader Nicolas Perrot who lived among the Indians of the Great Lakes for decades beginning in 1665 wrote: "dog flesh is ranked as the principle and most esteemed of all viands and they served it with several meats, as the flesh of the bear, the elk, or any other large game... in order to render this repast a solemn one, there must be a dog, whose head is presented to the most prominent warriors."

Antoine de le Mothe Cadillac described a feast of the dead at Michilimackinac (St. Ignace) that he witnessed while serving there as commandant in 1694-1697:

> *They kill a large number of dogs, which are to them what sheep are to us, and are valued by them more any other animal, and make a feast of them. But, before eating, they set up two great poles and fasten a dog to the top of them, which they sacrifice to the sun and the moon, praying to them to have pity and to take care of the souls of their relatives, to light them on their journeys, and to guide them to the dwelling place of their ancestors.*

Dogs were eaten at other important occasions as well. Ethnologist Frances Densmore recorded that among the Chippewa of the Upper Peninsula the final ceremony before the departure of a war party from a village was the dog feast. She wrote, "the head alone was eaten, and only the men who were going with the expedition partook of it."

Antoine Denis Raudot, intendant of New France from 1705-1710, wrote in his memoir of the Illinois tribe at the south end of Lake Michigan: "As the feast of dogs is the true war feast among the savages, the women take care to shut up all of those of the cabin, for as many as the warriors find at this time they kill to regale themselves."

More than one European fur trader who spent seasons with the Indians also learned to stifle affection for "man's best friend" and appreciate dog meat as a source of nourishment when needed. In 1791, John Long published a narrative of the 20 years he had spent trading with Great Lake Indians, during which he was adopted into the Chippewa tribe. While spending a hungry January in 1778 at aptly named Lac La Mort north of Lake Superior, he recorded: "We were compelled to kill a favorite dog... which most sensibly afflicted me, because independent of the attachment toward him, he was a very useful animal."

Other Europeans participated in canine cuisine, not out of hunger but because of the demands of aboriginal etiquette. Artist George Catlin, who immortalized western Indian culture on canvas and text during his travels in the 1830's, painted "the great dinner of dogs" during which he and several American government officials found themselves, though fear of offending their hosts, unable to refuse sampling. He described six large kettles of bubbling stew awaiting the feast. After each consumed a small helping "we all agreed the meat was well cooked and seemed to be well flavored and palatable food, and no doubt it could have been eaten with relish if we had been hungry, and ignorant of the nature of the food we were eating."

Catlin, one of few Nineteenth Century chroniclers who lived among and wrote of the Indians to achieve a genuine empathetic understanding of their seemingly savage culture, explained the true meaning of the dog feast:

> Among all Indian tribes the dog is more valued than among any part of the civilized world. The Indian has more time to devote to his company, and his untutored mind more nearly assimilates that of his faithful servant. He keeps his dog closer company, and draws him nearer to his heart. They hunt together and are equal sharers of the chase. Their bed is one. On rocks and on their coats of arms they carve his image as the symbol of fidelity. Yet the Indian will sacrifice his faithful follower, with tears in his eyes. He will offer him

In the 1830s, George Catlin sketched "A Great Dinner of Dog," a feast he was forced to participate in.

as a sacrifice to seal a sacred pledge of friendship he has made. Since a feast of venison or buffalo meat is due anyone who enters an Indian's wigwam, it conveys but passive or neutral evidence of friendship and counts for nothing. I have seen the master take from the bowl the head of his victim and talk of its former affection and fidelity with tears in his eyes.

So, it would seem, American Indians ate their dogs not became they considered them as mere livestock to be slaughtered at will, but because they valued them so highly their death was truly a sacrifice. It brings to mind the *Old Testament* story of Abraham preparing to sacrifice his oldest and dearest son.

Not all dogs sacrificed to propitiate the heavens were necessarily consumed. Observers recorded many instances of dogs being killed to appease the spirits during dangerous canoes voyages or when sudden storms threatened to swamp canoes. Prior to long voyages, Perrot wrote that the Chippewa "are careful to kill some dogs with their clubs, and to hang their bodies from a tree or pole, which they consecrate to the sun or the lake, in order to obtain fair weather."

English fur trader Alexander Henry recorded an adventure during a traverse of the Straits of Mackinac in 1793: "On our passage we encountered a gale of wind, and there was some apprehension of danger. To avert it, a dog, of which the legs were previously tied together, was thrown in the lake; an offering designed to sooth the angry passions of some offended Manito."

As late as 1831, Shiawassee County pioneer B.O. Williams observed some Chippewa deliberately drown a puppy while canoeing a dangerous stretch of the river. Favorite dogs of the deceased were also sometimes killed and buried with the body to accompany it to the next world. Jesuit Father Paul Le Jeune wrote in 1636 of an Algonquian Indian's desire to bury two dogs with his young daughter - which, of course, the priest denied as a pagan superstition. Another missionary, Father William Metzdorf, a laborer among the Great Lakes Potawatomi who had

In 1833, Swiss artist Karl Bodmer painted the interior of a Mandan lodge showing the close relationship between Indian and dog.

been removed to Kansas in the Nineteenth Century, discovered a variant use of dogs after burial of the dead:

> *Generally the body is only partly covered with logs or stones or earth. They then tie a dog near the grave, to keep watch over it. If he is able to get loose before he starves to death, and goes home, it is considered a good omen, a sign that the deceased has arrived happily at the great hunting-grounds, and does not need the dog anymore. Often, in passing by new graves, I made both dogs and people happy, by cutting the rope.*

While the custom of sacrificing and/or devouring man's best friend has become a thing of the past among American Indians, canine flesh remains a popular delicacy in the Orient from whence the American Indians are thought to have traversed the Bering Land Bridge eons ago. So as not to offend visitors with variant tastes the Chinese government, in fact, made a concerted effort to temporarily stifle dog menu items in restaurants, street vendors hawking dog delicacies and butcher shops offering puppy meat during the Olympics Games in Beijing.

And then there is the somewhat apocryphal story of a pair of Chippewa men who traveled from the Upper Peninsula to Chicago in 1893 to work as roustabouts at the Columbian World's Fair. Tired and hungry after their first day's work they spotted a big sign reading "Hot Dogs - 10 Cents." The first Indian slid his dime across the counter and said "hot dog." When given his order, he turned and shielded it from his friend. The second ordered the same, was served, and solemnly contemplating the food, grunted to his companion - "What part of dog you get?"■

A Chippewa family and dog sled as painted by W. Day in the 19th century. (courtesy Victoria, Canada, Archives)

XXV

1837 & 2008: CONTINUITY AND CHANGE

Like waves crashing against the beach, the years come and go. Sometimes storms reverberate across the decades and patterns emerge, repetition and transmutation, destinies linked and legacies formed. Eighteen thirty-seven was such a year.

On January 26, 1837, Michigan entered the Union as the 26th state. It had not been an easy transition from territory to statehood. Existing states to the south coveted Michigan's borderlands. Indiana gobbled away a slice when it became a state in 1817. Ohio lusted after the Toledo Strip, and, based on variant surveys, denied the territory statehood for more than two years. Only after armed militias nearly battled it out, and President Andrew Jackson temporarily removed Michigan's feisty young governor, Stevens T. Mason, was the conflict resolved in Ohio's favor. As compensation Congress awarded Michigan the western two thirds of the Upper Peninsula - a bad bargain many Michiganders thought at the time.

It was boom times for the infant state. The federal land office in Bronson, newly renamed Kalamazoo, set a record for sales in 1836 - 1,634,511 acres of prime Michigan forests, park-like oak openings and prairies purchased at $1.25 an acre - and the land rush continued into 1837. Bona fide settlers eager to

This tavern west of Detroit accommodated the rush of Michigan land-lookers during the 1830s.

cast their lot with the new state bought some of the land. But speculators intent on reselling at a tidy profit, grabbed up many choice tracts. And they paid for vast acreages largely with credit and/or worthless "wildcat bank" notes. Inflation spiraled upward. President Andrew Jackson's Specie Circular of 1836 required government lands to be purchased with hard money (gold or silver coins) and when it took effect the following year, the bubble burst.

The nation suffered a severe economic depression with Michigan the epicenter. The rush of new settlers dwindled, commodity prices crashed, many businesses went bankrupt and much of the land bought by speculators was ultimately lost to back taxes and foreclosures. Sound familiar?

In addition to the depression, other sections of the nation faced a variety of troubles in 1837. The Territory of Florida experienced a severe frost which entirely destroyed the citrus crop. That, in conjunction with a steep decline in the value of cotton, brought about the downfall of credit, and numerous Florida banks failed. Floridians responded by amending their constitution, making it unlawful for bankers to hold public office. Florida was also in the throes of the second Seminole War which ultimately cost the lives of 1,500 American soldiers. Led by wily Chief Osceola, the Seminoles repeatedly defeated American forces sent into the Everglades. On October 21, 1837, Gen. Thomas Jesup ruthlessly took Osceola prisoner while the chief was negotiating under a flag of truce. Confined in prison, the broken-hearted Indian died soon after, but the Seminoles fought on, not signing an official truce until 1934. Osceola's name is commemorated in Michigan as a county south of Cadillac.

It was in 1837 that the United States granted official recognition to a new nation - the Republic of Texas. Americans had begun colonizing the Mexican province of Texas in the 1820s, and they brought slaves with them . As more and more "Anglos" and their slaves flooded in, the Mexican Congress enacted a law prohibiting the immigration of any more in 1830. This eventually led to a declaration of independence from

George Catlin sketched Osceola in 1837.

Mexico in 1836, war, with Sam Houston as Texas commander, the Siege of the Alamo, the defeat of Gen. Antonio Santa Anna at the Battle of San Jacinto and creation of the Lone Star Republic. Texas petitioned for annexation to the United States in 1837, but largely because of opposition by antislavery forces, not until 1845 would Texas join the Union.

The slavery issue which would ultimately be decided by four bloody years of Civil War beginning in 1861 was further enflamed by a *cause celebre* in 1837 known as the Lovejoy Affair. Elijah Parish Lovejoy, a preacher and newspaper editor originally from Maine, published an abolitionist periodical in Alton, Illinois. Local pro-slavery mobs attacked and wrecked his print shop three times. On November 7, 1837, during a fourth attack, Lovejoy opened his front door and was mowed down by five bullets. The murder of Lovejoy created widespread excitement across the northern states. Numerous anti-slavery publications and speeches about the affair infuriated Southerners who feared that their human property might be lost. Owen Lovejoy continued his brother's campaign by openly violating an 1837 Illinois state law that prohibited public anti-slavery meetings.

And the year 1837 witnessed a important event across the Atlantic. Following the death of King William IV, a slender, attractive 18-year-old named Victoria came to the throne on June 20, 1837. Her reign, the longest in British history, would last until her death in 1901. Prim and proper, the personification of respectability and morality, she gave her name to an era when table legs were called limbs and items such as undergarments were termed "unmentionables." Proper Victorian etiquette decreed, according to one respected authority, that "the works of male and female authors be separated on bookshelves - their proximity, unless they happen to be married, should not be tolerated." In 1840, Queen Victoria married her cousin Prince Albert. When he died in 1861, her grief was inconsolable. For the remainder of her reign she wore only the black of a mourning widow, and she grew heavier and heavier.

Scroll ahead through the years past the speculative boom and subsequent financial panic of 1857. Stop in 1861 when the

A contemporary print of the pro-slavery mob's attack on Lovejoy's Alton, Illinois, newspaper.

dying Prince Albert very likely prevented war between Great Britain and the North which could well have altered the outcome of the Civil War. The prince toned down a strongly worded dispatch from the British government to Washington over the Union Navy's boarding the British steamer *Trent* and arresting two Confederate diplomats en route to London. Now, push forward past the financial panics of 1873, 1893, 1907 and the Great Depression of the 1930s.

Stop at the year 2008. Queen Victoria would not have been amused by the public auction of a pair of her unmentionables on July 30th. A happy Canadian collector paid $9,000 for the 50-inch waist knickers embroidered with the queen's royal monogram.

Later in the year came the bursting of the bubble of yet another credit crisis as Americans talked increasingly of foreclosures, stock market crash, depression and government bail-outs. Some things seem destined to never change. Others do.

Queen Victoria, shortly after assuming the throne in 1837.

As the year ended George W. Bush dusted off his hands after "just one of those presidencies" and prepared to return to his ranch in the "Lone Star State" and once again tackle brush-cutting. In November, voters had overwhelmingly elected a senator from the state that had outlawed even the public discussion of slavery in 1837 as the first African-American president of the United States. And that brings a pleasant symmetry to the years, 1837 and 2008. ■

SOURCES

Chapter 1   Michigan's First Christmas Celebration

Bigot, Vincent & Dablon, Claude. *Relation de ce… Norville France…*1679. in Thwaites, Reuben Gold, ed. *The Jesuit Relations & Allied Documents*. Cleveland, 1900. Vol. 61 p. 101-123.

Donnelly, Joseph P. *Jacques Marquette*, S.J. Chicago, 1968.

Douglas, George William & Compton, Helen Douglas. *The American Book of Days*. New York. 1965.

Dunbar, Willis F. & May, George S. Michigan: *A History of the Wolverine State*. Grand Rapids, [1980].

Hodge, Frederick Webb. *Handbook of the American Indians…* 2 Vols. Washington, 1912.

Havighurst, Walter. *Three Flags at the Straits*. Englewood Cliffs, N.J., [1966].

Kinietz, W. Vernon. *The Indians of the Western Great Lakes*. Ann Arbor, 1940.

Shea, John G. *History of the Catholic Missions Among the Indian Tribes…* New York, 1854.

Steck, Francis Borgia. *Marquette Legends*. New York, [1960].

Chapter 2   The Moore-Hascall Dream Machine

Cousins, Peter H. "That Shall He Also Reap." *Henry Ford Museum & Greenfield Village Herald*. N.D.

[Durant, Samuel]. *History of Kalamazoo County…* Philadelphia, 1880.

Higgins, F. Hal. "The Moore-Hascall Harvester Centennial Approaches." *Michigan History Magazine*. Vol. XIV (Summer, 1930). p. 415.

Prairie Historical Society Newsletter. Climax, Michigan. Vol. 21, Issue 6. (Nov.-Dec., 2005).

Quick, Graeme R. & Buckele, Wesley F. *The Grain Harvesters*. St. Joseph, Michigan. American Society of Agricultural Engineers, 1978.

Wilcox, Lucille V. "Hiram Moore & His Life's Work." Unpublished Term Paper for Dr. James Knauss's Michigan History Course at Western Michigan College. 1 Feb. 1941.

Chapter 3   Dr. Goodrich, Allegan County's Pioneer Physicians

Burr, C.B. ed. *Medical History of Michigan*. 2 Vols. Minneapolis & Saint Paul, 1930.

Eberle, John. *A Treatise on the Practice of Medicine*. 6th Edition. 2 Vols. Philadelphia, 1845.

Johnson, Charles B. *Sixty Years in Medical Harness*.... New York, 1926.

[Johnson, Chrisfield], ed. *History of Allegan & Barry Counties, Michigan*... Philadelphia, 1880.

Chapter 4   "The Wildest & Tenderest Piece of Beauty on God's Earth"

Fuller, Margaret. *Summer On the Lakes in 1843*. Boston & New York, 1844.

Huback, Robert R. *Early Midwestern Travel Narratives: An Annotated Bibliography. 1634-1850*. Detroit, 1961.

Jameson, Anna. *Winter Studies & Summer Rambles in Canada*. 2 Vols. New York, 1839.

Kenzie, Juliette. *Wau Bun*... New York, 1856.

Martineau, Harriet. *Society In America*. 2 Vols. Paris, 1837.

Massie, Larry B. "The Literature of the Mackinac Country," introduction to Williams, Meade C. *Early Mackinac*. Au Train, Michigan, 1987.

Pleasure's Pathway: Michigan Popular Resorts. Olivet, Michigan, [1891].

Steele, Eliza R. *A Summer Journey In the West*. New York, 1841.

Wood, Edwin O. *Historic Mackinac*. 2 Vols. New York, 1918.

Chapter 5   Talking with the Dead

Cadwallader, M.E. *Hydesville in History*. Chicago, 1922.

Centennial Book of *Modern Spiritualism in America*. Chicago, [1948].

Hardinge, Emma. *Modern American Spiritualism*. New York. 1870.

Underhill, A. Leah. *The Missing Link in Modern Spiritualism.* New York, 1885.

Whiting, R. Augusta. *Golden Memories of an Ernest Life: A Biography of A. B. Whiting.* Boston, 1872.

Chapter 6   Scientists in the North Country

Agassiz, Elizabeth Cary. *Louis Agassiz: His Life & Correspondence.* 2 Vols. Boston, 1885.

Agassiz, Louis & Cabot, J. Elliot. *Lake Superior…* Boston, 1850.

Bayliss, Joseph & Estelle. *Historic St. Joseph Island.* Cedar Rapids, Iowa, 1938.

Fowle, Otto. *Sault Ste. Marie & Its Great Waterway.* New York, 1925.

Lurie, Edward. *Louis Agassiz: A Life in Science.* Chicago, [1960].

Wright, Larry & Patricia. *Great Lakes Lighthouses Encyclopedia.* [Erin, Ontario, 2006].

Chapter 7   When Christmas Was Just Another Day

Diary entries are among the holdings of the Archives & Local History Collection at Western Michigan University.

Douglas: *American Book of Days.*

Rowland, O.W. *A History of Van Buren County, Michigan.* 2 Vols. Chicago, 1912.

Chapter 8   The Husseys of Battle Creek

Barnes, Charles E. "Battle Creek as a Station on the Underground Railroad." *Michigan Pioneer & Historical Collections.* Vol. 38 (1912), p. 279.

[Barnes, Georgene & White, Constance], eds. *Beyond These Gates 1844-1989.* [Battle Creek, 1989].

Biographical Review of Calhoun County, Michigan… Chicago, 1904.

Coffin, Levi. *Reminiscences.* Cincinnati, [1876].

History of Calhoun County, Michigan… Philadelphia, 1877.

Lowe, Berenice Bryant. *Tales of Battle Creek*. Battle Creek, [1976].
Michigan Biographies. 2 Vols. Lansing, 1924.

Chapter 9   The Drummer Boy of Chickamauga

Bak, Richard. *A Distant Thunder: Michigan In the Civil War*. [Ann Arbor, 2004].
Downey, Fairfax. *Fife, Drum & Bugle*. [Fort Collins, Colorado, 1971].
Faust, Patricia, ed. *Historical Times Illustrated Encyclopedia of the Civil War*. New York, [1986].
Heitman, Francis B. *Historical Register & Dictionary of the United States Army…* 2 Vols. Washington 1903.
Johnson, Robert U. & Buel, Clarence C., eds. *Battles & Leaders of the Civil War*. 4 Vols. New York, [1884].
Record of Service of Michigan Volunteers in the Civil War. Twenty-Second Michigan Infantry. [Kalamazoo, 1903].
Robertson, John, Compiler. *Michigan in the War*. Revised Edition. Lansing, 1882.

Chapter 10   Chaplain Corby of the Irish Brigade

Bilby, Joseph, G. *Remember Fontenoy! The 69th New York & the Irish Brigade in the Civil War*. Hightstown, New Jersey, 1995.
A Biographical History of Eminent & Self-Made Men of the State of Indiana. Cincinnati, 1880.
Corby, William. *Memoirs of Chaplain Life*. Notre Dame, Indiana, 1893.
Faust: *Encyclopedia of the Civil War*.
Final Report of the Battlefield of Gettysburg. 3 Vols. Albany, 1902.
Headley, J. T. *The Great Rebellion*. 2 Vols. Hartford, 1864.
History of the Catholic Church in Indiana. 2 Vols. Logansport, Indiana, 1898.
Hope, Arthur J. *Notre Dame: One Hundred Years*. Notre Dame, Indiana, [1948].
Kohl, Laurence Frederick & Richard, Margaret C., eds. *Irish*

Green & Union Blue. The Civil War Letters of Peter Welsh. New York.1986.

Chapter 11   Book Hawkers & Door Knockers

"Agents Wanted for Standard Works." J.B. Burr & Hyde. Hartford, Conn. (Broadside).
Atlas of Berrien County, Michigan. Chicago, 1885. (Prospectus).
Carson, Gerald, "Get the Prospect Seated and Keep Talking." *American Heritage.* Vol. IX. No. 5 (August, 1958). p.38
Dacus, J.A. "Canvasing Agents" in *A Guide to Success…* St. Louis, 1880.
Grand Rapids *Daily Times.* 9 June 1874. p.1.
Honsberger, Mrs. J. to F. L. Emery. Charlotte. 6 January 1892. (Manuscript letter in author's possession).
[Lewis, Charles B.]. *Quad's Odds…* Detroit, 1875.
Mortimer, J.H. *Confessions of a Book Agent.* Chicago, [1906].
Nelles, Annie. *The Life of a Book Agent.* 5th Edition Revised. St. Louis, 1892.
Parsons, W. F. & White, J.E. *Parson's Hand-Book of Forms.* Battle Creek, 1882. (Prospectus).
Rayne, Mrs. M.L. *What Can a Woman Do…* Detroit, 1883.
Smith, James L. *Michigan: The History of the Peninsula State From the Earliest Times.* Muskegon, 1909. (Prospectus).

Chapter 12   Agassiz Redux & Red Rock Riches

Agassiz, George A., ed. *Letters & Recollections of Alexander Agassiz…* Boston & New York, 1913.
Agassiz, Louis: *Lake Superior.*
Benedict, C. Harry. *Red Metal: The Calumet & Hecla Story.* Ann Arbor, 1952.
Gates, William B. *Michigan Copper & Boston Dollars.* Cambridge, Mass., 1951.
Lankton, Larry. *Cradle to Grave: Life, Work & Death at the Lake Superior Copper Mines.* New York & Oxford, [1991].
Murdock, Angus. *Boom Copper.* New York, 1943.
Peattie, Donald C. "Alexander Agassiz" in *Dictionary of American Biography.* Vol. 1. p. 111-114.

Perry, Bliss. *Life & Letters of Henry Lee Higginson*. Boston, [1921].

Thurner, Arthur W. *Calumet, Copper & People*. [Hancock, Michigan, 1974].

_____. *Strangers & Sojourns: A History of Michigan Keweenaw Peninsula*. Detroit, [1994].

Chapter 13   As the Bishop Saw It

Barbara, Sister Mary. *A Covenant With Stones*. Nazareth, Michigan, 1939.

Grapevine. Commemorative Issue. July 1989.

May, Katherine, compiler. "Historical Data Concerning Borgess Hospital." 1989-1917. unpublished typescript.

O'Brien, Rev. Frank A., ed. *"As the Bishop Saw It"*... Detroit, [1892].

Pare', George. *The Catholic Church in Detroit* 1701-1888. Detroit, 1951.

Swantek, Wanda. *The Sisters of St. Joseph of Nazareth 1889-1929: A Chronicle*. Nazareth, Michigan, 1983.

Tentler, Leslie W. *Seasons of Grace: A History of the Catholic Archdiocese of Detroit*. Detroit, [1990].

Chapter 14   Johnston's Got Your Bible

Atlas of Allegan County... Philadelphia, 1873.

Buechner, Cecilia Bain. *The Pokagon*. Indianapolis, 1933.

Clark, Edward B. *Birds of Lakeside & Prairie*. Chicago, [1901].

Farm Journal... Directory of Allegan County. 1916-1921. Philadelphia, 1916.

Halgren, Jeanne. *Casco Township Bounty By the Lake*. Douglas, Michigan, [1996].

Hulst, Cornelia Steketee. *Indian Sketches*. New York, 1912.

[James, Edwin], translator. *Kekitchemanitomenahn*... Albany, 1833.

Michigan State Gazetteer & Business Directory. Detroit, 1899.

Pokagon, [Simon]. *Queen of the Woods*. 3rd Edition. Hartford, Michigan, 1901.

_____. *The Man's Red Rebuke*. N.P., 1893.

Romig, Walter. *Michigan Place Names*. 2nd Edition. Detroit, 1986.
Semi-Centennial Reminiscences of the Founding of Holland, Michigan. N.P., 1897.
Thomas, Henry F. *A Twentieth Century History of Allegan County, Michigan*. Chicago, 1907.

Chapter 15   Autumn Ramblings in Northern Michigan

Heilman, Elizabeth Wiltbank. "Shields, George Oliver." *Dictionary of American Biography*. Vol. XVII. p. 106.
Hornaday, William T. *Thirty Years War For Wild Life*.... Stamford, Connecticut, 1931.
Jenkins, David H. & Bartlett, Ilo H. *Michigan Whitetails*. Lansing, 1959.
Mershon, William B. *Recollections of My Fifty Years Hunting & Fishing*. Boston, 1923.
Petersen, Eugene T. *Conservation of Michigan's Natural Resources*. Lansing, 1960.
Shields, G.O. *Rustlings in the Rockies*. Chicago, 1883.

Chapter 16   Big Heads & Bump Bunkum

Andrews, Thomas S. *Ira Andrews & Ann Hopkinson: Their Ancestors & Posterity*... Toledo, 1879.
Michigan State Gazetteer... Vol V. Detroit, 1881.
New Illustrated Self-Instructor in Phrenology... New York, 1880.
Sizer, Nelson. *Forty Years in Phrenology*... New York, 1882.
Stern, Madeleine B. *Heads & Headliners: The Phrenological Fowlers*. Norman, Oklahoma, [1971].
Weller, Charles E. *Yesterday: A Chronicle of Early Life in the West*. Indianapolis, 1921.

Chapter 17   When in Pain - Please Pass the Paine's - Hiccup!

Barton, Anna. *For Friendship's Sake*. Kalamazoo, 1882.
Bureau of the Census. Special Reports. Religious Bodies: 1906. 2 Vols. Washington, 1910.

Corey, Francis A. *Business Directory of Kalamazoo...* Vol. 12. Kalamazoo, 1893.
Holbrook, Stewart H. *The Golden Age of Quackery.* New York, [1959].
Mains, Lura A. *Zizpah: Autobiographical Sketches.* Grand Rapids, 1892.
Massie, Larry B. & Schmitt, Peter. *Kalamazoo: The Place Behind the Product.* Woodland Hills, California, [1981].
Our Album. [Burlington, Vermont, 1892].
The Paine's Celery Compound Annual [Burlington, Vermont, 1904].

Chapter 19   The Kid From Kalamazoo & Other Knights of the Road

Belknap, Charles E. *The Yesterdays of Grand Rapids.* Grand Rapids, 1922.
Burns, Roger A. *Knights of the Road: A Hobo History.* New York, [1980].
Cook, Joseph. *Boston Monday Lectures: Socialism...* Boston, 1884.
Davies, William H. *The Autobiography of a Super-Tramp.* New York, 1917.
_____. *Later Days.* New York, [1926].
Dunbar, Willis F. *How It Was in Hartford.* Grand Rapids, [1968].
Flynt, Josiah. *My Life.* New York, 1908.
_____. *Notes of a Itinerant Policeman.* Boston, 1900.
_____. *Tramping With Tramps.* New York, 1899.
Hair, Robert E. *Sturgis Michigan: Its Story to 1930.* Sturgis, 1992.
Hawkins, Mabel Hudson. *Glimpses of A 19th Century Village...* [Vicksburg, 1990].
Kelly, Edmond. *The Elimination of the Tramp.* New York, 1908.
Kunitz, Stanley & Haycraft, Howard. *Twentieth Century Authors.* New York, 1942.
Laws of the Territory of Michigan. Vol. 1. Lansing, 1871.
Milburn, George. *The Hobo's Hornbook.* New York, 1930.
Minehan, Thomas. *Boy & Girl Tramps of America.* New York, [1934].

Palmer, Friend. *Early Days in Detroit*. Detroit, [1906].
Phillips, Loren. *Songs of the Cinder Trails*. Shelbyville, Indiana, 1937.
Seibold, David H. *Grand Haven In the Path of Destiny*. [Dexter, Michigan, 2007].
Stark, George W. *In Old Detroit*. Detroit, 1939.

Chapter 20   Michigan's Better Angel

Brown, Forman. *Better Angel*. Third Revised Edition. Boston, 1995.
_____. *Punch's Progress*. New York, 1936.
_____. *Spider Kin*. Chicago, 1929.
_____. *Walls*. [Otsego, 1925].
Burklund, Carl E. ed. *New Michigan Verse*. Ann Arbor. 1940.
Otsego Union 1901-1960.
Smith, Larry. "A Remembrance of Forman Brown" The Puppetry Home Page (internet).

Chapter 21   The Roamer, "America's Smartest Car"

Advantageous Differences. Barley Motor Car Company. Kalamazoo, [1921].
Bell, Jack R. "Kalamazoo Made at Least 5 bids for Place in U.S. Car Industry." Kalamazoo *Gazette*. 30 May 1946.
The Double OK. Barley Motor Car Company. Kalamazoo, 1921.
Dunbar, Willis. "Those Were the Firms That Were." *Kalamazoo Magazine*. [April, 1965].
Georgana, G. N. *The Complete Encyclopedia of Motorcars 1885 to the Present*. New York, [1968].
Good Roads Included. Barley Motor Car Company. Kalamazoo, [1921].
An Honor Roll Containing a Pictorial Record of the War Service... Kalamazoo County 1917-1918-1919. Mrs. O.H. Clark, [1920].
New Amsterdam Theatre. New York. 27 May 1918 (Playbill).
Ryan, Dan. "Roamer Auto, Kalamazoo's Pride..." Kalamazoo *Gazette*. 8 January 1956.

Truesdell, Bill. "Roamer: Flashback to an Era of Elegance." *Kalamazoo Review*. 1975. p. 26.

Chapter 22   A Belated Rebuttal On Russia

Dykstra, Gerald O. *A Belated Rebuttal On Russia*. Allegan, [1928].

Perrigo, Blake. Oral Interview. Allegan. 1 October 1989.

Ross, Edward Alsworth. *The Russian Soviet Republic*. New York, [1923].

Chapter 23   Cass County's Crusading Correspondent

"Death of a Correspondent." *Time*. Vol. XXV. No. 20. (13 May 1940). p. 61 & 62.

Fisher, Frederick B. *That Strange Little Brown Man Gandhi*. New York, 1932.

Miller, Webb. *I found No Peace*. New York, 1936.

N.W. Ayer & Son's *American Newspaper Annual & Directory*. Philadelphia, 1915.

"Saints & Heroes - Of Truth & Shame." *Time*. Vol. LI. No. 6. (9 Feb. 1948). p. 24-26.

Stan, Louis M. "Miller, Webb." *Dictionary of American Biography*. 2nd Supplement.

Chapter 24   Old Bones & Canine Cuisine

Blair, Emma Helen. *The Indian Tribes of the Upper Mississippi Valley & the Region of the Great Lakes*. Reprint Edition. Lincoln, Nebraska, [1996].

Catlin, George. *Letters & Notes On the North American Indians*. 2 Vols. London, 1841.

Densmore, Frances. *Chippewa Customs*. B.A.E. Bulletin 86. Washington, 1929.

Dunbar & May: *Michigan*.

Greenman, Emerson R. "An Early Historic Cemetery at St. Ignace." *Michigan Archeologist*. Vol. 4 No. 2. (July 1959). p. 28-35.

Hodge: *Handbook of American Indians*.

Kinietz: *Indians of the Great Lakes*.

Wiedensaul, Scott. "Tracking America's First Dogs." *Smithsonian Magazine*. March 1999. p. 44-57.

Chapter 25   1837 & 2008: Continuity & Change.

Connolly, A.P. *The Nineteenth Century*. Chicago, 1900.
Dunbar & May: *Michigan*.
Florida: A Guide to the Southernmost State. New York, [1939].
Hall, Walter Phelps, et. al. *A History of England & the Empire - Commonwealth*. Waltham. Mass. [1961].
Illinois: *A Descriptive & Historical Guide*. Chicago, 1939.
Knudson, J. "Queen Victoria's Underwear Sold at Auction." (Internet) 31 July 2008.
Massie, Larry "Plows, Ships & Shovels: Economic Development in Michigan. 1836-1866" in *Michigan: Visions of our Past*. East Lansing, 1989.
Morris, Richard B., ed. *Encyclopedia of American History*. Sixth Edition. New York, [1982].
Somervell, David C. "Victoria" in *Encyclopedia Britannica*. 14th Edition. London, [1929]. p. 121-130.

INDEX

Abbey, P.L. 196
Abolitionist Movement 100
Adams, George C. 92
Addrup, Germany 150
Adrian 100, 200
Africa 186
Agassiz, Alexander 80, 138-147
Agassiz, Anna 140, 141, 143, 145, 147
Agassiz, Cecile 139
Agassiz, Louis 72-81, 138-140
Albany, New York 86, 156
Albert, Prince 264, 265
Albion 69, 100
Albion College 235
Alexandria, Virginia 116
Algonac County 184-193
Allegan 36, 37, 39, 211, 233, 237
Allegan County 34-39, 86, 156, 158, 223
Alpena 187
Alton, Illinois 264, 265
American Fur Company 44
Andersonville, GA. 111
Andrews, Annie 181
Andrews, Thomas S. 181
Ann Arbor 100, 215, 220, 222, 249
Antietam, Battle of 117
Appomattox Courthouse 111
Arlington National Cemetery 112
Ascot Speedway 230
Astor, John Jacob 44
Atlanta, Georgia 124
Au Sable River 172

Baber, Vaughn 96
Bailloquet, Pierre 17
Baker Furniture Co. 233
Bandini, Bob 230
Bangor 200
Barley, Albert C. 224-232
Barley Manufacturing Co. 225
Barley Motor Car Co. 226-232
Barton, Anna 202
Batvia, Ohio 170
Battle Creek 69, 95-104, 136

Bay City 151, 184, 187, 200, 215
Beaven, James 51
Bedford 186
Beery, Wallace 224
Belfast, Ireland 152-154
Belknap, Charles 208, 209
Belleau Woods, Battle 245
Benton Harbor 242
Berrien County 91, 128, 158, 211
Berrien Springs 84, 91, 200
Bertrand, Joseph 158
Bickley, Samuel 175
Big Mac from Mackinaw 215
Big Rapids 183, 187
Blakeman & Gibbs Co. 69
Blarney Castle, Ireland 154
Blood, Charles 226
Blood, Maurice 226
Bodmer, Karl 257
Borgess, Caspar 149-154
Borgess Hospital 149, 154, 155
Boston 140-142, 179, 208, 220
Bowen, Sarah Eddy 98
Brady, Hugh 50
Bragg, Braxton 109
Branch County Jail 211
Brandon, Richard 220
Braun, Alexander 139
Braun, Maximillian 139
Britten, Rollo 244
Bronson 260
Bronson, Titus 24
Brooklyn 64
Brooks, George M. 48, 49
Brown, E. Lakin 28
Brown, Edwin A. 210
Brown, Forman 217-223
Brown, George R. 220
Brown, Pet 220
Brule, Entienne 15
Burr Oak 84
Buffalo, New York 46, 69, 74, 98, 186
Bugdan, Rose 161
Bull Run, Battle of 117

Burbank, E.A. 159
Burlington, Vermont 195, 196, 199
Burnett, Harry 220
Burt lake 172
Burtt, Frank 228
Butterfield, Clara 199

Cabot, James Elliot 74, 76, 80
Cadillac, Antoine de la Mothe 22, 253
Calhoun County 186
California 30
Calumet 143-145, 148
Calumet & Hecla Mine 138, 141-147
Camp, J. 200
Camp California 116
Canada 100, 102
Cannon, Warren B. 228
Cape Breton Island 186
Cape Horn 30
Catherwood, Mary H. 60
Catlin, George 254-256, 263
Carnegie, Andrew 240
Caruso, Carla 142
Casco Township 156, 161
Cassopolis 100, 240
Cass County 87, 102, 158, 239
Cayuga County, New York 98
Cayuga Lake, New York 98
Celery Medicine Co. 196
Centennial Heights 145
Ceresco 69
Chamberlain, Neville 245
Champlain, Samuel 15
Chancellorville, Battle 120
Charles L. Webster Co. 128
Charles II 86
Charlotte 133
Chase, A.B. 166
Chateau-Thierry, Battle 245
Cheboygan 172, 186, 220
Chevrolet, Louis 230
Chicago 46, 69, 126, 128, 135, 160, 161, 212, 242-244, 258
Chicago Military Road 46
Chickahomeny Swamp 117
Chickamauga, Battle of 105-112

Chippewa tribe 52, 253, 254, 256, 258, 259
Cincinnati, Ohio 99, 151
City of Berlin 154
Civil War 71, 89, 105-124, 170, 196, 208, 264, 265
Christmas, Holiday 13-23, 82-94
Claddagh, Ireland 149
Clark, Deputy 212
Clem, Johnny 105-112
Clemenceau, Georges 239
Climax 30, 33, 100
Climax Prairie 25
Coffin, Levi 99, 100
Coldwater 211, 215
Colorado 97
Columbian Exposition 160, 161
Columbus, Ohio 151
Comstock Township 92
Con the Sneak from Battle Creek 215
Connecticut 37
Constellation 54
Cook, Joseph 208
Cooper 84, 89
Cooper, Harry 212
Cooper, James Fenimore 30
Cooper Township 82, 84
Corby, Daniel 114, 115
Corby, William 113-123
Craig, John 212
Crooked Lake 172
Cross, John 100
Cross Village 149
Custer, George A. 179, 180
Cuvier, Georges 74

Darwin, Charles 73, 74, 80
Davies, William H. 204, 205, 211
Day, Philetus 89
Day, W. 259
Daytona Beach, FL. 229, 230
DeLano, Ephraim 82
DeLano, George 82, 89, 94
DeLano Family 86
Delaware 232
Densmore, Frances 253

Denton, Prof. 84
DeTour 76
Detroit 22, 23, 43, 46, 50, 69, 70, 98, 100, 114, 115, 124, 126, 127-131, 149, 151, 154, 181, 201, 208, 210, 215, 261
Detroit Fatty 204, 205, 215
Detroit River 100
Dexter 100
Dharasana, India 245
Diamond Lake 241
Dickens, Charles 86
Dillon, James 115, 116
Disney, Walt 109
Doolittle, Charles 107
Dousman, Michael 48
Dowagiac 239, 240, 242
Doyle, Arthur Conan 71
Dressler, Marie 220
Dublin, Ireland 152
Dunbar, Willis 211
Dunkley, Samuel J. 198, 199
Dykstra, Garrit 232
Dykstra, Gerald O. 233-237
Dykstra, Lillian 237
Dykstra, Martha 233

East Abington, Mass. 62
East Bridgewater Academy 64
East Saginaw 186
Eastland 241-144
Earl, Charles 84
Earl, Edna 91
Earl, Nancy 91
Earl, Sandford 84
Earl, Stephen V. 84, 89, 91
Eliot, Charles W. 142
Elmira 167, 171, 172
Ely, Elisha 36
Emerson, Ralph Waldo 56
Emery, Laban D. 133
England 42, 86
Engle, Washington A. 84, 94, 159, 160, 163, 164
Enjalran, Jean 13-23
Epiphany, Holiday 17

Erie Canal 24
Essen, Germany 150
Ethiopia 245

Fair Oaks, Battle of 117
Fairbanks, Douglas 220
Falmouth, Virginia 118
Farini, Giovani 69
Farley, Benjamin 84
Featherstonhaugh, George W. 45
Ferris, Woodbridge N. 183
Ferris University 183
Ferry, Amanda 44
Ferry, William 44
Fisher, A.W. 200
Fisher, Clarence 200
Fisher, Demott 200
Fisher, Florence 201
Fitzmorris, Charles 242
Fitzmaurice, John W. 184-193
Flint 175, 177, 187
Florida 170, 262
Flowerfield Township 26
Flynt, Josiah 212
Ford, Frank 126
Ford, Henry 228
Ford, Prof. 84
Fort de Buade 22
Fort Holmes 46, 48, 56
Fort Michilimackinac 76
Fort Pontchartrain 22
Fort St. Joseph 78
Fort Sumter 105
Fort Winnebago 43
Foster, John Wells 57, 138
Fowler, Lorenzo 179
Fowler, Orson 179, 181, 183
Fox, Catherine 67, 68
Fox, Margaretta 67, 68
Fraker, H.J. 200
Francisco 100
Frost, Robert 220
Fuller, Charles 226
Fuller, Frank 226
Fuller, Sarah Margaret 53, 55-58

Gall, Franz J. 179
Galway, Ireland 149
Gandhi, Mahatma 239, 245-248
Garbo, Greta 220
Geddes 100
Genesee County, New York 24
Genesee Prairie 24
Germany 89
Gettysburg, Battle of 113, 120-123
Giles, Eugene 124, 125
Glasgow, Scotland 235
Glendale 199
Goodspeed, Leland F. 230
Goodrich, Osman D. 34-39
Goodrich, Osman E. 39
Goose Island 76
Gouin, M.V.
Grand Haven 211
Grand Army of the Republic 128
Grand Rapids 71, 131, 181-183, 187, 208, 209
Grand Rapids & Indians Railroad 167
Grand River 181, 250
Grant, Ulysses 109, 128, 160
Grass Lake 100
Great Depression 215
Greeley, Horace 56
Green Bay 43, 46
Greenman, Emerson F. 249, 250
Gros Cap 80
Gulf of St. Lawrence 186

Hall Brothers 196
Halstead, D.W. 200
Hallowell, Benjamin 95
Hascall, Volney 30
Hamilton, Ontario 186
Hamilton, William B. 109
Haner, Sally 91
Harbor Springs 149
Harris, Frank 220
Harrison, Carter 161
Hartford 84, 94, 159, 211
Hartford, Conn. 128
Harvard University 140, 142, 147, 179
Hascall, John 24-33

Hascall, Mary 24, 26, 26, 32
Hastings 200
Hawkhead 161, 162, 166
Hawkhead, William 161
Hawkins, Mabel 212
Headley, John T. 117
Henry, Alexander 76, 256
Hitke, Kurt 230
Hitler, Adolph 239
Hogmire, Calista 202
Holland 89, 163
Holland, W.J. 135
Hollywood 222, 224
Honsberger, J. 133
Hooker, Joseph 120
Hoskins, Sarah 194, 195, 202
Houghton, Douglass 138
Houston, Sam 264
Hubbard, Gurdon 249
Hubbard Lake 184
Hulbert, Edwin J. 141, 142
Humbolt, Alexander 74
Huron County, Ohio 36
Huron Tribe 13-23
Hussey, Susan 99, 102
Hussey, Erastus 95-104
Hussey, Sarah 95-104
Hydesville, New York 67

Illinois 43, 97
Illinois Tribe 253
India 245-248
Indiana 100, 135, 260
Indianapolis 500 230
International Bridge 78
Iowa 97, 170
Irish Brigade 113-123
Iroquois Confederacy 17, 22

J.B. Burr & Hyde Co. 128
Jackson 99, 100
Jackson, Andrew 260
Jackson, Charles T. 138
Jackson, Stonewall 120
Jackson County 64
Jesuit Order 15-23

Jesuit Relations 13, 20
Jesup, Thomas 262
Johnson, Charles B. 36
Johnson, Mary 175, 177
Johnson, W. J. C. 177
Johnston, Adelbert 161
Johnston, Theron 156-166
Joliet, Louis 15
Joos, Edward 149
James, Edwin 156
Jameson, Anna 50-54

Kalamazoo 24, 30, 69, 82, 96, 133, 149, 150, 152, 154, 155, 181, 196, 198, 199, 202, 211, 212, 224-232, 260
Kalamazoo County 24-33, 82, 86, 92, 94
Kalamazoo Kid 215
Kalamazoo Looseleaf Binder Co. 232
Kalamazoo Medicine Co. 196
Kalamazoo Realty Co. 230
Kalamazoo River 218
Kane, Grace F. 60
Kansas 181
Keaton, Buster 224
Keesee, Dennis M. 109
Kelly, Edmond 205
Kentucky 102, 107
Keweenaw Peninsula 138, 140-148, 181
Kibbie 166
Kings County, Ireland 114
Kinzie, John 43-44
Kinzie, Juliette 43
Kress, Ella 201, 202

Lac La Mort 254
Lafitau, Joseph 14, 21, 251
Laframboise, Madam 44
Lake Erie 24, 98
Lake Erie Steamboat Line 43
Lake Geneva, Switzerland 151
Lake Huron 15, 16, 76
Lake Michigan 37, 44, 220
Lake St. Clair 151, 154
Lake Superior 17, 44, 72-80
Lakeshore Push 212
Lakeview 172

Lanchester, Elsa 222
Lapeer County 107
Laurium 143
Lawrence, Eveline 87,89
Lawrence, Levi 87
Lawrence Scientific School 140
Le Cage, Louis 230
Lee, Gypsy Rose 220
Lee, Robert E. 95, 117
Lee Township 156, 163
Le Jeune, Paul 256
Lenin, Nikolai 237
Leningrad 235, 236
Leoni 100
Les Cheneaux Island 76
Lewis, Charles B. 129, 130
Lexington, Kentucky 138
Liberty Party 99
Lime Island 76
Lincoln, Abraham 105, 114
Little Big Horn, Battle 180
Little Prairie Ronde 87
Littlejohn, Flavius 252
Livingston County 107
Livonia 69
Lloyd George, David 239
London, England 226, 245-248
Lonesome Lou from Kalamazoo 215
Long, John 254
Los Angeles, CA. 220, 223, 230
Louisiana 30
Louisville, Kentucky 167
Lovejoy, Elijah P. 264, 265
Lovejoy, Owen 264
Lyon, Lucius 26, 30

Macatawa 220
Mackinac Bridge 249
Mackinac Island 15, 40-60, 74-76, 172, 220
Macomb County 107, 111
Madeline Island 15
Magill, Juliette 43
Maine 97, 264
Manistee 220, 244
Marengo 69

Marion, IN. 224
Marquette 187
Marquette, Jacques 15, 16, 78
Marshall 69, 95, 100, 102, 200
Martineau, Harriet 40, 42, 46-49, 60, 179
Mary 172
Mason, Stevens T. 260
Massachusetts 74, 86, 87, 97, 140
Mauntel, J.B. 149, 152
McCain, Mrs. 71
McClellan, George 119
McCoskry, Samuel A. 50
McGregor, Tracy 211
McGregor Mission 211
McKenney, Thomas 42
Meagher, Thomas Francis 116, 117, 120
Menominee Tribe 52, 55
Merritt, William G. 95, 103, 104
Mershon, William B. 168
Metzdorf, William 256, 258
Meuse-Argonne, Battle 245
Mexico 244, 262
Meyer, Richard 223
Michigan Automobile Co. 226
Michigan Buggy Co. 228
Michigan Center 100
Michigan Central Railroad 187
Michigan Free Employment Bureau 211
Michigan Soldiers Home 208
Michigan Southern & Lakeshore Railroad 212
Michigan State University 25
Michilimackinac 253
Midler, Bette 223
Milford 71
Miller, Charlotte 239
Miller, Jacob 239
Miller, Webb 239-248
Milwaukee, 46, 49
Minehan, Thomas 215
Mission San Jose 30
Mississippi River 15, 44
Mitchell, David 46
Monroe 149, 180
Montmorency County 168-172
Montreal, Canada 114

Moore, Andrew Y. 25, 30, 31
Moore, Hiram 25-33
Moore, Oliver 30
Moscow, Russia 235, 237
Mud Lake 78
Mullett Lake 172
Mulholland, St. Clair 122
Munich, Germany 74
Munich Conference 245
Munuscong Lake 78
Muskegon 128, 185, 220
Mussolini, Benito 239

Nazareth Academy 154
Nelles, Annie 124-137
New France 15
New Hampshire 25
New Harmony, IN. 87
New Hartford, New York 36, 43
New Haven, Connecticut 220
Neuchatel, Switzerland 139
New York 87, 95, 175, 179
New York City 54, 115, 219, 226, 235
Newark, Ohio 105, 112
Niagara, Ontario 186
Nicolet, Jean 15
Niles 103, 126
Nippissing Tribe 17
Norman, Frederick 185
North Carolina State College 220
Northern Belle 172
Notre Dame, Indian 115, 158
Notre Dame University 122, 123
Nouvel, Henri 17

Oak Openings 30
Oakland County 107, 111
Oberlin College 158
O'Brien, Francis 149-152
Ocqueoc River 189
Ohio 107, 186, 260
Ohio River 100
Oklahoma 23
Ontario 186
Oneida County, N. Y. 36
Orleans County, N.Y. 86

Osceola 262, 263
Osceola County 262
Oscoda 187
Oshtemo Township 24-33
Otsego 84, 217-221, 223
Ottawa County 212
Ottawa Tribe 15, 19, 20, 52, 158, 163, 250

Page, Lorena 60
Paine, Mrs. 196
Paine's Celery Compound 194-203
Pakistan 248
Paris 245
Paris, France 13, 74, 226
Parkman, Francis 141
Parma 100
Paw Paw 194, 195, 202
Pennsylvania 87, 140, 215
Peoria, Ill. 135
Peoria County, Ill. 135
Perrigo, Blake 237
Perrot, Nicolas 253, 256
Pershing, John 239, 244
Petersburg, Battle 120
Petoskey 172, 220
Phelps, Edward E. 196
Phillips, Loren 215
Pickford, Mary 224
Pius IX, Pope 151
Plymouth 100
Plymouth Township 98
Point Iroquois 80
Pokagon 158, 239, 248
Pokagon, Leopold 157
Pokagon, Simon 156-166
Polar Bear Division 235
Pollard, E.A. 135
Pontiac 107
Portage, Wisconsin 44
Potawatomi Tribe 52, 157-166
Prairie Ronde 24, 28
Presque Isle County 189
Prettyman, Nancy M. 200

Quaker Church 95-104

Quality Drug Stores 196
Quebec 15
Quingo, Julia 159

Railroad Jack 212, 213
Ransom, Epaphroditus 30
Raudot, Antonine Denis 253
Rayne, M.L. 127, 131-133
Recollet Order 15
Red Jacket 143, 147
Republican Party 99
Resaca, Battle of 176
Reynolds, George 84, 86, 91
Rhode Island 97
Rhodes, James A. 109
Richardson, A.E. 196
Richardson, Earl 249
River Raisin 66
Rochester, N.Y. 26, 28, 67
Rogers City 189
Rome, Italy 152
Roscommon 187
Rosecrans, William S. 109
Rush Lake 165, 166
Russell, Anna 140, 141, 143
Rutenber Motor Co. 225

San Antonio, TX. 112
Saginaw 168, 187
Saginaw Slim 204
St. Clair County 107, 111
St. Dominic Church 165, 166
St. Ignace 13-23, 249, 250, 253
St. Joseph 242
St. Joseph County 84, 91
St. Joseph Island 76
St. Joseph River 158
St. Louis 128
St. Marys Rapids 72
St. Patrick's Day 118-120
St. Xavier College 151
San Francisco 30
San Jacinto, Battle 264
Sand Creek 185
Sanilac County 107
Santa Anna, Antonio 264

Sarles, Roscoe 229, 230
Saugatuck 220
Sault Canal 80
Sault Rapids 54, 80
Sault Ste. Marie 15, 52, 54, 58, 74, 76, 78-80, 138, 156
Sault Ste. Marie, Ontario 78
Schoolcraft 100
Schoolcraft, Henry Rowe 52, 54
Schoolcraft, Jane 52
Schoolcraft Township 24, 94
Scio 100
Sears, Robert 61
Seminole War 263
Seven Days Campaign 117
Shaw, Quincy A. 141, 143
Shepardson, Charley 91
Sheridan, Philip 180
Sherman, Mary 71
Shiawassee County 256
Shields, George Oliver 167-174
Shiloh, Battle 109
Shugart, Zachariah 102
Sinagaw, Lonidaw 158, 164, 165
Sioux Tribe 20
Sizer, Nelson 179
Slavery 95-104
Smith, James L. 128
Smith, Lillie 84
Smith, William Alden 167
Sorin, Edward 115, 122
South America 80
South Bend, IN. 115, 242
South Dakota 97
South Haven 156, 166
Soviet Union 233-237
Spanish Civil War 245
Specie Circular of 1836 262
Spurzheim, Johann G. 179
Stalin, Joseph 237
Stalingrad, Russia 235
Stapleton, Elizabeth 114
Steele, Eliza 54-56
Stockbridge, Francis B. 199
Straits of Mackinac 13-23, 40, 46, 256
Streator, IL. 225, 226

Streator Motor Car Co. 225
Stuart, Elizabeth 43
Stuart, Frank 94
Stuart, Robert 43
Sturgis 212
Swartzburg 100
Swedenborgian Church 87
Switzerland 73

Taft, William Howard 224
Tamarack 143
Tanner, John 156
Territorial Road 46
Texas 262, 264
3rd Ohio Infantry 107
Thomas, George H. 109, 112
Thoreau, Henry 239, 247
Three Rivers 91, 257
Thunder Bay 43
Ticharetzkaya, Russia 233
Toledo, Ohio 69, 212
Toledo Strip 260
Topinabee 158
Torch Lake 145
Toronto, Ontario 50, 186
Trent 265
Turnabout Theatre 222, 223
Twain, Mark 128
22nd Michigan Infantry 105, 107, 110, 111
Twin Lakes 168
Twinsburg, Ohio 158
Tyler, G.W. 194

U.S. Patent Office 26, 27, 30
Underground Railroad 95-104
University of Michigan 36, 84, 215, 219, 220, 222, 235, 237, 244, 245, 249

Van Buren County 158, 166, 199
Verdun, Battle 245
Vicksburg 212
Victoria, Queen 89, 264-266
Villa, Poncho 244
Virginia 95
Virginia Peninsula 117

Volinia Township 87
Volstead Act 196

War of 1812 78, 86
Warner, Beers & Co. 128
Washington, D.C. 160
Washington, George 87
Watertown, Wisconsin 122
Wayne County 98,99
Wayne County, N.Y. 86
Webster, Daniel F. 50
Webster, Edward 50
Weller, Charles E. 181
Wells, Richardson & Co. 195-199
Wells, Samuel 179
Wells, William 196-199
Western Michigan University 82
White, Stewart Edward 71
Whitehall 185
Whiting, Albert B. 62-71
Whiting, R. Augusta 71
Whiting, Rachel 62
Whitney, Josiah D. 57, 138
Wigginton, George P. 232
Wilder, Jerfferson J. 199
Wildman, Eddie 97
William, IV, King 264
Williams, B.O. 256
Wilson, Woodrow 244
Windsor, Ontario 100
Winnebago Tribe 52, 55
Wisconsin 30, 43, 97, 170
Wise, M.J. 200
Wisner, Moses 107
Woolson, Constance F. 60
World War I 226, 235, 245, 246
World War II 245
Wyandotte County, KS.
Wyandotte Tribe 23

Yale Puppeteers 220
Ypsilanti 100, 201